I have crisscrossed the globe for over four exciting decades, ministering to people from every background and walk of life. Pat Schatzline's book *Why Is God So Mad at Me?* answers a universal question I have heard over and over again throughout the years. Granted, people word it differently, but their hearts ache with the twisted fear that God has failed them, forgotten them, or forsaken them. Pat gives straightforward, biblical and yet compassionate answers to this universal dilemma. He paints a powerful picture of the unending love of God. Many of us have secretly asked Jesus how far we'd have to go to get beyond His love's reach. As reflected in Pat's book, the Lord reminds us all that *we can't* go far enough to exhaust His love—because if we ever got to the end of His arm, the only thing left for us to do would be to fall into a nail print!

—JEANNE MAYO
YOUTH PASTOR, SPEAKER, AND AUTHOR
PRESIDENT, YOUTHLEADERSCOACH.COM

Pat Schatzline has written an incredibly detailed and touching examination of the principles of God's love. He has shown through Scripture as well as his own experiences that many of the popular conceptions about God simply aren't true. A spirit of failure is the greatest enemy of this new generation of believers, and this book will help to do away with those negative misconceptions. For an inspiring reaffirmation of the possibilities God has for your life and the reasons He pushes people to do greater things, you must read this book.

—MATTHEW BARNETT
COFOUNDER, THE DREAM CENTER
LOS ANGELES, CA

We live in a day when the enemy has brought m___ _ ___ g arguments into the minds of a _____ _____ l love of an awesome God. The tive with guilt and held other zline has such a unique pers answer these lies of the enemy. _____ ____ ___ ___ and having touched countless lives, he has been qualified by heaven to speak on behalf of the truth. Get ready to be set free from confusion and released into the God-given destiny on your life as you read this book.

—Joel Stockstill
Teaching Pastor, Bethany World Prayer Center
Director 220 Internship (bethany.org)
Baker, LA

In this captivating book Pat has gone deep into the hidden places of the heart, where insecurity and fear keep us from fully receiving the perfect love of our heavenly Father. Through Pat's passion and authenticity the Holy Spirit is able to reveal to us the greatest, most profound truth ever known to man: "Jesus loves me, this I know. For the Bible tells me so." Thank you, Pat, for awakening the childlike faith in all of us.

—Karen Wheaton
Evangelist, The Ramp (theramp.org)
Hamilton, AL

Pat Schatzline has written a book that is going to touch the very core of people who are asking the tough questions. I believe this message is a mandate from God to touch this generation in their heart. I am excited to see the impact of this book.

—Benny Perez
Lead Pastor, The Church at South Las Vegas
Henderson, NV

Pat Schatzline, international evangelist and pastor, compiles years of biblical and practical knowledge to openly answer the private question, "Why is God so mad at me?" Let Pat's life experiences guide you on the road to understanding. Break from your past and move to your future. Your healing begins on the first page.

—Glen Berteau
Pastor, Calvary Temple Worship Center (ctwc.com)
Modesto, CA

With incredible sensitivity Pat takes the reader on an awesome journey into the amazing heart of God. With great thoughtfulness and purpose he addresses some of life's hardest questions. Read this book, and be prepared to fall in love with Jesus all over again.

—JIM RALEY
LEAD PASTOR, CALVARY CHRISTIAN CENTER
ORMOND BEACH, FL

Pat Schatzline courageously asks the question hovering just beneath the surface of American faith. While consumer Christianity endeavors to redefine and reshape the image of God, Pat skillfully reminds us of the loving nature and intent of God toward people. As an evangelist and pastor Pat shoulders the suffering and disappointments encountered daily, but through this book he practically and wonderfully redirects our souls toward tangible hope. This book is a game-changer! It asserts healing energy into the wounds of America's damaged soul.

—JIM HENNESY
SENIOR PASTOR, TRINITY CHURCH (TRINITYCHURCH.ORG)
CEDAR HILL, TX

Pat Schatzline is my friend and covenant brother. And while we do not have the liberty to meet as regularly as we want to, each time we meet there is such a bond that I can only describe it as a kingdom connection. Pat has cleared the misconception that God is always angry and distant, that He sits as a judge waiting to punish at the first hint of disobedience. This is something that has pervaded the minds of many believers. In Asia especially many are raised in homes where they rarely have any experience of their father's love or touch. The orphan spirit has hindered many believers, young and old alike, from entering into the richness of an intimate walk with our heavenly Father. Pat Schatzline's book has done a marvelous work in addressing these misconceptions. I believe this book will set many free from the intense battle with the spirit of failure and will restore the image of God.

—YANG TUCK YOONG
SENIOR PASTOR, CORNERSTONE COMMUNITY
CHURCH (CSCC.ORG.SG)
SINGAPORE

If we truly understood how much God loves us, we would never be the same. In his book *Why Is God So Mad at Me?*, Pat Schatzline provides an insightful and detailed look at man's desperate struggle with the truth of God's amazing, unconditional love. I am confident that Pat's book will resonate with you as it did with me and that you will find the wisdom shared here to be life changing.

—DR. DAVE MARTIN
AUTHOR OF *THE TWELVE TRAITS OF THE GREATS*

I have known Pat Schatzline for a number of years and have heard him speak in numerous contexts. He is a powerful verbal communicator. Now he brings that gift of communication to the printed page. *Why Is God So Mad at Me?* is a must-read for every believer. It corrects modern-day theological myths about God. It addresses the issue of self-esteem vs. pride. I've put this book on my must-read list for any believer, regardless of how many years he's been saved.

—EVON G. HORTON, BA, MDIV, DMIN
SENIOR PASTOR, BROWNSVILLE ASSEMBLY
(BROWNSVILLEAG.ORG)
PENSACOLA, FL

Pat Schatzline is a voice to be heard when it comes to this crucial global question being asked by millions: Why is God so mad at me? Pat was obviously in touch with those who cried out from their daily tormented lives to be able to articulate this outstanding cry of desperation. Thank you, Pat, for listening to humanity's cry. The enemy's agenda is to paint a picture with lies that make God look like the one who is mad. He is not an angry God but a God of intense, pure love. The idea that He is mad is a demonic attack on the spotless character of our Savior Jesus Christ and the redemption He brought to us on the cross.

This book is not another echo but an urgent voice answering the desperate cry that needs to be heard. This passionate release from Pat Schatzline will reveal the true heart of our heavenly Father, and the passion He has for humanity will be felt as you read these pages. I believe this book could be instrumental in changing the question in a dramatic way as the God of love is revealed. The question could soon be, "Why is this God who died on a cross so in love with me that He forgives my sins and gives me eternal life?" The lie of the enemy will be outshined by the truth of the gospel. I truly believe this book, coming from the heart of Pat, will be instrumental in setting the record straight. Many will receive emotional, mental, and spiritual healing by reading this book.

—ANDRE VAN ZYL
AUTHOR AND EVANGELIST
GOOD NEWS TO THE NATIONS (GNNI.ORG)
DACULA, GA

Pat Schatzline has heard the troubled heartbeat of a wounded generation, and God has given him a response. *Why Is God So Mad at Me?* will bring healing and answers to a culture that has been bruised by Satan but has mistakenly blamed God. This book is a message of hope and understanding to those whose lives have become ensnared in a trap of pain and misplaced anger. I believe this book has a strategic message that will introduce searching people to the heart and character of our loving, gracious God. Read this book, share this book, and pray that God will connect this book to those who need this message so desperately.

—GEORGE SAWYER
FOUNDING PASTOR, CALVARY ASSEMBLY OF GOD
DECATUR, AL

Like a doctor who *diagnoses* his patient and then prescribes medicine to help eliminate a sickness, Pat Schatzline has received from the Holy Spirit one of the most revealing diagnoses of a major deception in the body of Christ and among unbelievers. In his new book, *Why Is God So Mad at Me?*, Pat shows us the root cause of this misconception and then skillfully presents the cure. This is a must-read for every believer, a lifetime manual for healthy spiritual growth.

—AL BRICE
SENIOR PASTOR, COVENANT LOVE CHURCH (CLFC.COM)
FAYETTEVILLE, NC

When Pat Schatzline says, "God is not mad at you—He's mad about you," he speaks the true heart of the unconditional love God has for His creation! How sad that for far too long we have concentrated on how bad we are rather than on how good God is. God's grace is still more powerful than sin and triumphs over it. As you read Pat's wonderful book *Why Is God So Mad at Me?* perhaps you will discover…He's not!

—DAVID THOMAS
LEAD PASTOR, VICTORY CHRISTIAN CENTER
(VCCCOITSVILLE.COM)
YOUNGSTOWN, OH

Pat Schatzline is a noted evangelist, gifted communicator, and talented writer. In his new book, *Why Is God So Mad at Me?*, Pat draws from his experiences in marriage, as a dad, and as a communicator who has touched the hearts of thousands of individuals. Pat, through an obvious grasp of real-life issues, brings thought-provoking answers to tough questions in a practical and scriptural manner. Pat does not spare the details from his own life. You will learn from this author about his struggles, his victories, and his failures. This book is written from a refreshingly honest and transparent perspective. Read *Why Is God So Mad at Me?* with a pen, notebook, and box of tissues at hand.

—BRET ALLEN
SENIOR PASTOR, BETHEL CHURCH (BETHEL.ORG)
SAN JOSE, CA

Pat's open heart and clear *message* of freedom are as relevant in the rural areas of the South as in ultra-urban environments such as San Francisco. This book's message hits this generation at the point of its greatest need. Then it points the pathway to freedom. In a word, this book is *unbelievable!*

—Forrest Beiser
Lead Pastor, Glad Tidings Church (gtsf.org)
San Francisco, CA

Every generation needs to *understand* the father heart of God. Pat Schatzline has a tremendous gift for conveying the strength and covenant heart of our amazing, loving Father. If you know anyone who is struggling with whether God is angry or a loving Father God, this is the book to open his or her heart to a powerful truth that everyone needs to hear.

—Matt Berry
Executive Pastor and Communicator, Inspire Church
(inspirechurch.org)
Sydney, Australia

It is said of King David that "he served his generation well." I believe the same can be said of Pat Schatzline. He is a powerful, articulate, and clear voice to this generation. Pat Schatzline's book *Why Is God So Mad at Me?* has captured the essence of what the Lord is trying to speak to a generation—that, truly, God isn't mad but rather madly in love with people, with a generation. That truth is exemplified not only by this book but also in the ministry and life of Pat and Karen Schatzline. In this book you will find the answers to questions that have been asked for generations. Not only will the book answer those questions, but the truths and concepts conveyed in these pages also will set people free to experience the love of God. I cannot recommend this book strongly enough. It is a must-read.

—Donald L. Gibson
Senior Pastor, Mercy Gate Church
(mercygatechurch.com)
Mount Belvieu, TX

I have known Pat Schatzline for more than twenty years, and he is one of the most passionate communicators I have ever had speak to our youth. He preaches with a passion that is authentic and anointed, and his message is relevant to real-life issues. *Why Is God So Mad at Me?* communicates to this lost, hurting generation a clear message of who God is and the fact that He is madly in love with them. Many students come to our statewide events. Again and again we see that this is the message this generation so desperately needs to hear.

If you are wondering if this book will be a good read, it will be more than that—it's a life-changing read. When so many speakers are merely echoing what has already been said, I believe Pat is a voice that speaks clearly and directly to the issues this generation faces. When life is filled with so many questions, books like this one provide hope and purpose. I recommend this book to students, leaders, pastors, parents—anyone who simply needs to hear the answer to the question, "Why is God so mad at me?"

—AL FORCE
YOUTH DIRECTOR, PENINSULAR FLORIDA DISTRICT COUNCIL
OF THE ASSEMBLIES OF GOD
LAKELAND, FL

Gangs, drug addiction, and illicit sexual activity—I am a witness to the sad deterioration of a generation that is desperately crying out for the love of a father. We are living in times when there is even a lack of spiritual fathers within the church. Pastor Pat is not only one of the most down-to-earth individuals I know, but he is also an amazing spiritual father to many—which is why this book was so hard to put down. The message in *Why Is God So Mad at Me?* is evidence that my good friend Pat Schatzline has heard the Father's heart. This book carries such a loving and profound revelation regarding the Father's love that I am certain it will transform any reader, of any age, forever.

—PATTY VALENZUELA
LEAD PASTOR, IGNITE MOVEMENT (IGNITEMOVEMENT.ORG)
EL PASO, TX

Why Is God So Mad at Me? is long overdue. Pat Schatzline lays out a concise clarion call to awaken a generation to an authentic love relationship with God! Generation transformation will happen through this book! Count on it!

—Paul Owens
Senior Pastor, FreshStart Church (freshstartaz.com)
Peoria, AZ

Pat Schatzline has never been one to shy away from tackling the tough issues. In this book he touches on a spiritual disease that has infiltrated the hearts of many of the people sitting in churches today. Whether you grew up in a pastor's home or on the streets, every person needs to read this book! It exposes the root of the question "Why is God so mad at me?", which has been planted in the hearts and minds of people of every age by the very powers of hell. For years Pat has effectively brought a proven prophetic voice to this generation, and this book is no different. It reveals the true heart of God. Pat encourages us to reframe our thought process and lean in to what Jesus is speaking to His church.

—Steve Mason
Youth Director, Alabama District Council of the
Assemblies of God
Montgomery, AL

Pat Schatzline's book *Why Is God So Mad at Me?* addresses a core misconception about the nature of God that both believers and nonbelievers wrestle with. As a pastor I've heard countless people describe the atrocities happening all around them as acts of God. Each time I hear that, I want to scream, "God has nothing to do with it!" Pat, in this book, artfully unveils the true nature and character of God in a world of madness.

—Jeremy Saylor
Lead Pastor, Christian Life Church (clcbham.com)
Birmingham, AL

This is an excellent book to open hearts and give insight to the unconditional love of the Father. As Pat unfolds God's Word, he enables you to discover and understand the Father's love. The relationship with the Father that is shared and related through the experiences of the Schatzline family and others will convince you that "God is not mad at you—God is mad about you!"

—Rev. Keith Elder
Legacy Ministries (legacies4leaders.com)
Billings, MT

This new book by Pat Schatzline provides a much-needed treatment of the subject of God's love. Aimed at addressing the idea of whether God is "mad at us," the book hits the target with answers to questions we all have. Providing a refreshing perspective on tragedy, hardship, and difficulties, the book helps readers remember—or discover for the first time—a love that is greater than can be imagined.

—Sean Cherry
Lead Pastor, The Summit Church at Birmingham
(thesummitbham.com)
Trussville, AL

I am blessed to be Pat's dad. He is not a person who lives for acclaim—he simply loves God and people! His passion is always intense. He writes to encourage people to reach their individual destiny, and this book will do just that.

—Dr. Patrick M. Schatzline
Founding Bishop, Daystar Ministries International
Northport, AL

If there ever was a person who deserved to grace the front of the youth ministry "Wheaties" box, it would be Pat. He once again cuts to the heart of a crucial need in our student culture and answers the question "Why is God so mad at me?" Pat provides exactly what an individual needs to know in a well-written and easy-to-understand format. In so doing, he has written an instant classic for those yearning to find answers.

—John Dougherty
District Youth Director, The Georgia
Assemblies of God
Macon, GA

Pat Schatzline is a great man with a high calling. *Why Is God So Mad at Me?* is timely for our world today. With so many challenges facing us, it is alarming that people are turning from God or becoming angry with Him rather than running to their Father. Pat addresses the very deep questions and concerns people have, and he does so in a clear, concise, and noncondemning way. This book will give you hope, build your faith, and restore you to a loving Father who simply wants relationship with His creation.

—TED MILLER
LEAD PASTOR, CROSSROADS CHURCH (CROSSROADSSOKC.COM)
OKLAHOMA CITY, OK

In his book *Why Is God So Mad at Me?*, Pat confronts a paradigm in culture that has a crippling potential in the church and in our world. Without a proper understanding of God's love and mercy, we will never understand His correction. Pat has done a masterful job of communicating the love that Paul explains in Ephesians 3:19, which is known beyond simple knowledge. This is at timely word that will resonate deep in the heart of the church and a generation.

—ROB SPERTI
WORSHIP AND PRAYER PASTOR,
WINSTON-SALEM FIRST ASSEMBLY
WINSTON-SALEM, NC

Do you know who your heavenly Father is? The truth is, you will never know your true identity and potential until you know your Father God and how much He believes in you. *Why Is God So Mad at Me?* by Pat Schatzline is a must-read. This book will show you who God your Father is and in turn will help you see your own identity in Him. This book had me in tears as I came to a new revelation of God as my Father. No matter where you are in life, you need this book. The majority of us, at one time or another, has asked, "Why is God so mad at me?" Throughout this book Pat shows with brilliant clarity not only who God is but also that He absolutely is not mad at you. What a freeing truth!

—JEREMY DONOVAN
PASTOR, SEVEN YOUTH MINISTRIES, CLAREMORE, OK
AUTHOR OF *THE HARD WAY*

Sometimes the circumstances in our lives feel so overwhelming, and they can leave us grappling with real emotions and real tough questions. If you or someone you know has a lot of those pesky unanswered tough questions, get this book! Pat answers those questions for you! As I read this book, I fought my own tears because what is in these pages touched things deep in my heart. Everyone needs to know this message. Get ready. Your life is about to be changed.

—HAZEM FARRAJ
HOST, *REFLECTIONS*

Why Is God So Mad at Me? by Pat Schatzline is a masterpiece in proving who God really is to humanity. This well-researched book from a seasoned communicator expounds on God's unconditional love for humanity while exposing the misconception that pain and suffering are the result of God's anger with us. This is a must-read for all Christians at any stage of their walk with Christ, especially those in ministry to others.

—DAVID GARCIA
LEAD PASTOR, GRACE WORLD OUTREACH CHURCH
BROOKSVILLE, FL

WHY IS GOD SO MAD AT ME?

DISPELLING THE LIES MANY PEOPLE BELIEVE

PAT SCHATZLINE

CHARISMA
HOUSE

Cover design by Gearbox Studio
Design Director: Bill Johnson

Visit the author's website at http://www.mercyseatministries .com, www.whyisgodsomadatme.com.

Library of Congress Cataloging-in-Publication Data:
Schatzline, Pat.
  Why is God so mad at me? / Pat Schatzline. -- 1st ed.
     p. cm.
  ISBN 978-1-61638-966-6 (trade paper) -- ISBN 978-1-61638-967-3 (e-book)
  1. God (Christianity)--Attributes. 2. God (Christianity)--Wrath. I. Title.
  BT130.S33 2013
  231--dc23

                                                2012036704

While the author has made every effort to provide accurate telephone numbers and Internet addresses at the time of publication, neither the publisher nor the author assumes any responsibility for errors or for changes that occur after publication.

First edition

13 14 15 16 17— 9 8 7 6 5 4 3 2 1
Printed in the United States of America

*To Karen, Nate, Abby, and Adrienne—
without you I would not have been able to
write this book!*

*Karen, my beautiful wife, you are my best
friend, my teacher, and my confidante. You
truly are amazing to me. Through your
grace, love, and purity you have shown me
how to be a man who chases after the heart
of God. You have taught me the meaning
of Christianity and the joy of walking in
the call of God. I love you with all of my
being. You have been used by God to change
a generation of girls and young ladies.*

*Abby, Nate, and Adrienne—you are our
gifts from God. I love you more than life. I
am so blessed to be your dad, friend, and
biggest fan. The three of you will change the
world for Jesus. Dream the impossible and
always know God handpicked your destiny.
I am so proud of you.*

CONTENTS

Part 4: Awaken to New Life

ACKNOWLEDGMENTS

To my amazing parents, Drs. Pat and Deb Schatzline—because of your God encounter when I was just a child, our family was transformed. You truly are my heroes! Your relentless pursuit of God, knowledge, and love has pushed me to always believe intimacy with Jesus is where life begins! Our family is simply a miracle from heaven!

To my dear brother, Pastor Scott Schatzline—thank you for your purity of life! God has used you over and over to remind me that faith in God is always full of wonders!

To my mother- and father-in-love, John and Gail Brown—you have taught me the joy of trusting God and always walking in freedom. I truly honor you!

To all of the former and current students and staff of the Forerunner School of Ministry—thank you for believing in the vision and helping to make Jesus famous. We love you and are honored to be spiritual parents to you. The heart of our ministry is to disperse champions for Christ. Go change the world!

To my assistant, Jamie Kowalski; Dr. Connie Lawrence; and my editors Debbie Marrie and Adrienne Gaines of Charisma House—thank you for your incredible patience and hard work to help get this message out to the world!

Final acknowledgements: I have always had a deep desire to thank the key voices in my life, those who have been purposeful in relationship and the ones positioned from afar to help bring transformation. I must list just a few of these great influencers who have walked with me up close and from a distance: Pastor Glen Berteau, Pastor Paul Owens, Pastor Jim Hennesy, Pastors Sam and Jeanne ("Mom") Mayo, Pastor Larry Stockstill, Evangelist Reinhard Bonnke, Pastor George Sawyer, Pastor Al Brice, Apostle David Thomas, Pastor Barry Danner, Pastor Jerry Parritt, Pastor Yang Tuck Yoong, Pastor Evon Horton, Pastor Jim Raley, Prophet Cindy Jacobs, Pastor Rocky McLendon, Mr. Steve Fox, Pastor Al Force, Mr. Jeff Martin, Evangelist John Bevere, Pastor Russell Evans, Pastor Forrest Beiser, Evangelist Andre Van Zyl, Pastor Sean Cherry, Pastor Jeremy Johnson, Pastor Michael Williams, Evangelist Karen Wheaton, Evangelist Jayme Montera, Pastor Keith Elder, Pastor James Ruddy, Pastor Stephen Stoner, Pastor Daniel Chua, Pastor Joe Iannone, Pastor Kurt Steinbach, Pastor Jeremy Saylor, Pastor Donald Gibson, Pastor Brian Dean, Pastor Rick Ross, Pastor Mark Ivey, Pastor Rich Wilkerson, Pastor Johnny Honaker, Pastor Tim Black, Pastor Tom Crandall, Pastor Mark Correll, Pastor Marty Burroughs, Pastor Brett Allen, Pastor Don Nordin, Pastor Mike York, Pastor Keith Daugherty, Pastor Jeremy Donovan, Pastor Ron Crum, Mr. Tim Roberts, Mr. Randy Howell, Pastor Dan Holbrook, Evangelist Allen Griffin, Pastor Sieg Krueger, Pastor Alex Pratt, Pastor Steve Sparling, Pastor Clem Salerno, Evangelist Gary Sapp, Pastor Doug Sayers, Pastor Andy and Patty Valenzuela, Pastor Sam Luke, Pastor Denny Duron, Pastor Murray Kelley, Pastor Jim Clark, Pastor Jon Russell, Pastor Rusty Nelson, Pastor Randel McCarty, Pastor Gail Craig, Pastor Mike Dillman, and Pastor David Garcia. Thank you for being Jesus with skin on! You have been my example to grow by, and you have made ministry fun!

FOREWORD

P AT SCHATZLINE IS an amazing evangelist. He has a big "antenna," an awesome analytical mind, and a heart full of God's compassionate love. He hears people, and he hears God. People ask all the time, "Why is God mad at me?" *Wow!* That is the wrong question. Mad? After God gave His only begotten Son to die for our salvation? Others are asking, "Why does God allow suffering?" God does not "allow" suffering. Do doctors allow sickness or the police allow crime? God is against sickness and the works of the devil. He sent Jesus to destroy them.

To understand sickness, for example, we have to learn that there is a universal disturbance of the order of God to which we all contribute. Personal sin makes us more vulnerable to the prevailing conditions of evil, so that a sickness could well be linked with our own failure. In Christ's day the sad masses believed afflictions branded them as sinful. This added to their distress. Jesus showed them that He was forgiving and caring. Guilt could be lifted from their consciences to give them the peace of heaven in their souls.

Pat's book deals above all with the solutions to life's questions and problems. They are found in Jesus Christ. He can, will, and does succeed—every time we allow Him to take over. I highly recommend this book.

—REINHARD BONNKE

Reinhard Bonnke, DD, is founder of the international ministry Christ for all Nations. Since the early 1980s Bonnke has conducted citywide meetings across Africa with as many as 1.6 million people in attendance in a single meeting. At the time of this writing the ministry had documented 68 million decisions for Christ since they started recording registered decision cards in 1987.

FOREWORD

As Christians called to change the world, our mandate is to represent Jesus in the earth, to give a clear picture of His heart and who He is. Too many people hold an inaccurate view of God that hinders their ability to fully come to Him and see Him for who He really is. God is a Father extravagantly in love with people and in passionate pursuit of a relationship with them. We must shout this from the rooftops to a world that is desperate for His love, and Pat Schatzline has done an incredible job of this in his book *Why Is God So Mad at Me?* The Lord has raised Pat up to be a voice for a generation and bring them into the arms of a Father who is not mad at them but is zealously in love with them. I believe when that issue is settled in the hearts of a generation, an awakening will explode in the nations of the earth.

—Banning Liebscher

Banning Liebscher and his wife, SeaJay, are on staff at Bethel Church in Redding, California, as the directors of Jesus Culture, a ministry dedicated to mobilizing a generation to shape culture and transform nations.

INTRODUCTION

I F GOD HAS the whole world in His hands and if He knows every hair on my head, then why do I always feel so far from Him? Could it be that God is mad at me?" I have heard that question over and over during my twenty years in ministry. In the early years I simply would tell people, "God isn't mad at you—He loves you!" But after ministering to hundreds of thousands of people and hearing the same thing again and again, I began to realize how widespread this thinking is. Millions of people from all backgrounds have bought into the idea that God is not only angry but also that He's angry with them. This belief is damaging countless lives, and I believe God has given me a mandate to set the record straight.

It was the summer of 2010, and I was in Florida with my family. In just a few days I would be launching into a ministry tour where I would be speaking at nineteen conferences and churches across the nation. But on this day I was planning to just rest with my family before my schedule became hectic. I got up early that morning to go for a jog, and while I was running, I suddenly heard God say, "Son, why do they think I am mad at them?"

The question stopped me for a minute, and I asked God what He meant, though I felt I knew what He was trying to tell me. Just days before two different pastors and two different students had spoken those exact words to me. As I continued to jog, God spoke to me again. He said, "Pat, they think I am mad at them. My very image has been tarnished, and I need you to set the record straight. Pat, tell them the truth about Me." I began to weep as I was jogging.

My mind started to race as I thought about all the people I knew who believed at one time or another that God was mad at them. I remembered when my grandmother, who was a godly woman, was diagnosed with lung cancer. After she received the doctor's report, she said to me, "I think God must be mad at me." Then I thought about a phone conversation I'd had with my sister, Renee, four years ago. She had given her life to Christ at our church just two weeks earlier, and as we were talking about all of the tough times she had faced, she told me, "Most of my life I felt God was mad at me."

Renee passed away suddenly two weeks later, and I thank God she knew she would be walking into the presence of a loving God. I will share with you in more detail how God used my sister to impact me very deeply. She died knowing God truly loved her, but I honestly believe that for most Christians, only when they walk into heaven will they at last realize what a loving and wonderful God we serve.

A few days after that encounter while jogging, I began to pen the message "Why Is God So Mad at Me?" It is the sermon from which this book was birthed. I believe this book is going to help many people finally understand the relentless, unfathomable love of the Savior. But first we have to unpack why so many believe God is mad at them. I must tell you that I spent many years feeling that way myself. For years I battled a very intense spirit of failure. I honestly believe that is the number one spirit that attacks this generation, and I will address that issue later in this book. We will look at nine reasons people believe God is mad at them—the biggest one being the way they perceive their earthy father.

My prayer is that no matter what your age, race, or economic background, this book will help you discover the real God! Oh, by the way, I want to warn you that in the process of reading this book you may experience supernatural miracles of God. We have seen many supernatural healings since I began sharing this message around the world.

There is a very real attack on the mind and emotions of this generation that is causing many people to cut themselves. Research shows that about 1 percent of the US population, which is between two million and three million people, exhibit some type of self-abusive behavior. And it is estimated that one in every two hundred girls between the ages of thirteen and nineteen—or one half of 1 percent—cut themselves regularly.[1]

I have traveled across the United States, South America, and as far as New Zealand, and I have seen cutters literally around the world. Self-injury is a cry for help that it is usually caused by intense emotional distress, anxiety, fear, insecurity, or anger. Cutting can be very addictive, but the miracle is that cutters have seen their scars disappear in the services where I have shared this message or while watching it on TV or the Internet. I recently asked the Lord, "Why are these types of miracles happening?" I felt Him speak to my heart and say, "Son, when the Father heals the inside of a person, it manifests on the outside!"

So I say, let the healing begin! I also want to warn you that when you start to go deeper in God, your flesh will always scream, "You don't belong here!" Don't listen to that voice. Remember, God demands pursuit not perfection. He doesn't need you to have never made mistakes or to have all the answers—He just wants you to seek Him with all your heart. He's not mad at you—He's mad about you. He's madly in love. Don't believe me? Just keep reading.

PART 1
THE GOD MISCONCEPTION

Chapter 1

A CULTURE FULL OF NOISE

THERE IS A passage in Isaiah that is almost impossible to believe. In it the Lord declares: "'I'm promising now no more anger, no more dressing you down. For even if the mountains walk away and the hills fall to pieces, my love won't walk away from you, my covenant commitment of peace won't fall apart.' The God who has compassion on you says so" (Isa. 54:9–10, THE MESSAGE).

No more anger. No more dressing you down. My love won't walk away from you. I often wonder how, with promises such as these in Scripture, so many people can believe God is angry with them. But the fact is, the noise from the culture is simply overwhelming. In fact, it can be absolutely deafening. It seems today that everyone is an expert on the subject of God.

German philosopher Friedrich Nietzsche is responsible for helping to start the noise. In the late 1800s he pronounced that "God is dead" in his famous book *The Gay Science*.[1] After this declaration secular humanism took off at lightning speed. Since Nietzsche's death more than a hundred years ago, his humanistic philosophy has only continued to spread.

Nietzsche and other heretical voices throughout history have, over time, done their very best to devalue God and who He is in our culture. As I have studied the lives of early humanists, I've been amazed at how many of them came from

1

deeply religious backgrounds. For example, Nietzsche's father was a Lutheran pastor,[2] and at one time Nietzsche attended the University of Bonn as a theology and philology student.[3] Yet somewhere along the way he, like so many others, lost his faith.

It is a dangerous thing to declare there is no God. The psalmist said it best, "Bilious and bloated, they gas, 'God is gone.' Their words are poison gas, fouling the air; they poison rivers and skies; thistles are their cash crop" (Ps. 14:1, THE MESSAGE). Nevertheless the poison of the secular humanistic agenda has worked its way from the university to the White House, from the courtroom to small-town city councils, and it has redefined the way this generation thinks.

Author Josh McDowell recently tweeted that "only 6% of this generation even believes that moral truth is absolute."[4] In other words, 94 percent of this generation believes truth is in the eye of the beholder. "Don't force me to believe something is fact," they say, "because my opinion, my feelings, and my history define my truth!" Adding to the noise coming from politics and education is the mainstream media's constant attack on our nation's concept of God. At times I hear statements about God or religion in the media, and I wish so badly I could set the record straight. News pundits scream their opinions of God as if they are absolute truth. Whether it is Disney, Nickelodeon, ABC, NBC, ESPN, or the twenty-four-hour news channels, it seems Christian values are always under assault. In 2005 James Dobson, founder of Focus on the Family, correctly observed in a *Time* magazine article that "we're involved in what is known as a culture war that is aimed right straight at the institution of the family."[5]

There was a time when people's views about God and truth were shaped at home, largely by their parents. But that is no longer the case. Today there are six Ps shaping how our nation, schools, churches, and families think about who God is, how

He feels, and what He does to get our attention. Those six Ps are:

- Parents
- Peers
- Politicians
- Pundits
- Professors
- Preachers

Those six Ps have influenced culture in so many ways it's difficult to calculate their impact. For many of us our early definitions of God came from at least three of the Ps: our parents, peers, and pastors. But with marriages dissolving at the fastest pace in history and the absence of fathers who lead their households, there is a lost sense of family values in most homes. According to author Tony Zuniga, in the 1950s the top five influences in a child's life were: parents/home, church, school, friends, and television. Today this is the list of the top five influences in a child's life:

1. Friends
2. TV
3. Parents/home
4. School
5. Church[6]

Their peers shape the way people think about everything from sexuality to addictions to what's right and wrong. And that's not good. An article about peer pressure gave this list of possible effects: "Peer pressure can lead to a loss of individuality.... You tend to blindly imitate the masses; you adopt their tastes of fashion, clothing, hair, music and general living. Peer pressure can actually lead you to lose your tastes of life and force yourself to begin liking what they like. Peer pressure is the human tendency to join the bandwagon, in which, the person loses his/her original way of looking at life."[7]

GOD MISCONCEPTIONS

The older we get, the more professors, politicians, and media pundits begin to influence us. In fact, nationwide the university campus is currently the greatest proponent of what I call "God misconceptions." Most university professors are sociological humanists. Students head off to college, and their very concept of God changes almost as soon as they take their first class. They listen to professors espousing atheism and humanism for hours each day; then the indoctrination continues for two, four, or six more years of higher education.

Because of colleges' incredible influence on young people, atheist groups are no longer hiding in closets on university campuses. According to the *New York Times*, anti-God groups are growing at a faster rate on college campuses than evangelical organizations. The *Times* reported that the student-led atheist group called the Secular Student Alliance has 146 chapters, up from 42 in 2003.[8] What's more, there has been a decline in the percentage of people in the United States who claim to be Christians while the number of those who claim no religious affiliation is on the rise. According to the American Religious Identification Survey, those who claimed "no religion" was the only group that grew in all fifty states in the last eighteen years.[9]

This is because the noise of the culture has helped to misconstrue people's view of God. They either see Him as impotent or they think He doesn't exist. Of course, thinking something about God doesn't make it true. One of my favorite quotes is from apologist C. S. Lewis, who wrote in his book *The*

Problem of Pain, "A man can no more diminish God's glory by refusing to worship Him than a lunatic can put out the sun by scribbling the word 'darkness' on the walls of his cell."[10]

One huge example of the way truth is being tarnished in our culture is the popularity of the view that all religions lead to God. The idea is that no matter what god you serve, it all works out in the end because all religious paths lead to the same god. This simply is not true. In John 14:6 Jesus said, "I am the way and the truth and the life. No one comes to the Father except through me." And again in John 6:44 He said, "No one can come to me unless the Father who sent me draws him, and I will raise him up at the last day."

I am reminded of the number one bumper sticker in America. Symbols from the major world religions spell out the word *coexist*. The C is the symbol for Islam, the O is the symbol for peace, the E is the symbol for males and females, the X is the symbol for Judaism, the I is dotted with a Wiccan pentangle, the S is the symbol for the yin-yang representing Confucianism, and the T is a cross, the symbol for Christianity.[11]

What most do not understand is that this view is actually Hinduism, which declares that all religions lead us to the same goal of serenity and paradise. I have seen this bumper sticker all over the world. With so many nations at war it is understandable that peace and harmony among the various faiths would be encouraged. But that bumper sticker is not really saying, "Can't we all just get along?" It is saying all religions are the same.

Yet the more I studied that bumper sticker, the more I saw how God could use it to change lives. It starts with Islam, the religion practiced by the children of Ishmael, and it ends with Christianity, the religion practiced by the descendants of Isaac, the children of promise. It starts with a crescent and ends with a cross. In other words, you can try all of these other religions, but sooner or later everything ends at the cross. Romans 14:11 says, "It is written: 'As surely as I live,' says the Lord, 'every knee will bow before me; every tongue will confess to God.'" The "noise" coming at this generation is overwhelming. That is why we must raise our voices to share the ultimate Truth.

HOW AMERICANS VIEW GOD

A recent book titled *America's Four Gods*, written by Baylor University professors Paul Froese and Christopher Bader, is an in-depth study of how Americans view God. With the help of the Gallup organization, thousands of people were interviewed. The findings were remarkable. Roughly 5 percent of respondents identified themselves as atheists, but after analyzing the rest of the results, the professors surmised that America has four main views of God.

1. *The Authoritative God.* Some 31 percent of Americans believe God is both engaged in the world and judgmental, meaning He will use any way to get our attention and wake us up.

2. *The Benevolent God.* Twenty-four percent of respondents believe God is engaged in our daily life, yet nonjudgmental.

3. *The Critical God.* Some 16 percent of those surveyed said God is judgmental and disengaged from our lives.

4. *The Distant God.* Twenty-four percent believe God is nonjudgmental but also disengaged from our lives.[12]

By studying the landscape of belief in America, the authors ascertained that roughly 95 percent of Americans believe in God. But believing in God isn't the same as knowing Him. I have to wonder how many people surveyed perceive God to be an awesome and holy Savior. I have to wonder how many have ever heard God calling their names. I wonder how many of them have felt the touch of His Spirit. God reveals Himself through His Word and His Spirit. He doesn't reveal Himself only to a special few. He is calling out to all of us, wanting us to awaken to Him. And you know what? Our spirits cry out to know Him.

The spirit of a man searches past his intellect and knowledge to discover his Creator. First Corinthians 2:10–13 tells us: "It was to us that God revealed these things by his Spirit. For his Spirit searches out everything and shows us God's deep secrets. No one can know a person's thoughts except that person's own spirit, and no one can know God's thoughts except God's own Spirit. And we have received God's Spirit (not the world's spirit), so we can know the wonderful things God has freely given us. When we tell you these things, we do not use words that come from human wisdom. Instead, we speak words given to us by the Spirit, using the Spirit's words to explain spiritual truths" (NLT).

God is not moved by opinions or polls. He speaks through His Word and His servants, and to our spirits through the Holy Spirit. He still speaks to His creation!

It is my goal in this book to give proof of who God really is to humanity. It would blow our minds if we truly understood how incredible our Creator is. The problem is, we have allowed others to define God. It is so easy to believe God is mad at you simply by listening to what others have declared.

But look at what the prophet Micah said about God: "Where is the god who can compare with you—wiping the slate clean of guilt, turning a blind eye, a deaf ear, to the past sins of your purged and precious people? You don't nurse your anger and don't stay angry long, for mercy is your specialty. That's what you love most!" (Mic. 7:18, THE MESSAGE). I love that verse. Mercy is God's specialty—not wrath or pain, but mercy!

I believe with all my heart that if we truly want to change the world, we will have to be faithful to the walk God has placed in front of us. If we don't stand for something, we will fall for anything. Together we can prove who God truly is and what He wants to do for His people. We must get back to God's specialty, which is love, compassion, repentance, and a life of victory.

My personal mantra has always been, "love without reason and holiness without compromise." My prayer is that this book will revolutionize your mind and heart concerning the things of God. I believe right now that He, the living and awesome God, is calling out to you!

Chapter 2

THE TRUTH ABOUT
NATURAL DISASTERS

IT SEEMS EVERY day there's news of another natural disaster. You've probably seen the headlines: "Thousands dead because of earthquake" or "Hundreds dead because of tornado!" Now that you understand how our nation views God, it is easy for you to see why many believe natural and man-made disasters must be from heaven. You can see why so many find it easy to believe that natural disasters must be due to God's anger with the nations. God must be simply stirring the ocean, blowing the wind, and stomping the earth in a rage. He must be judging our sins! He must be mad at us. This is another area where the noise of the culture can overwhelm the truth about God.

In the Old Testament God did judge nations. He led the nation of Israel into captivity for over four hundred years because of their rebellion and idolatry. We know Sodom and Gomorrah were destroyed because of their sexual perversion and lawlessness (Ezek. 16:49–50). God had planned to do the same with the city of Nineveh, but Jonah arrived in time to preach the word of the Lord. The people repented, and God spared the city (Jon. 3).

God does judge, but what we must understand is that His mercy and love prevail in the tough times. God warned Israel in Jeremiah 18:5–10 saying, "Like clay in the hand of the potter, so are you in my hand, O house of Israel. If at any time I announce that a nation or kingdom is to be uprooted, torn down and destroyed, and if that nation I warned repents of its evil, then I will relent and not inflict on it the disaster I had planned. And if at another time I announce that a nation or kingdom is to be built up and planted, and if it does evil in my sight and does not obey me, then I will reconsider the good I had intended to do for it."

Did you catch the key word in the last sentence? God plans *good* for the nations. God loves every nation and calls out to them to serve Him. He is their refuge. He always made a way of escape in the Old Testament, but because the world was under the law, as a just God He had to punish the nations when they were disobedient. Consider the admonition in Psalm 2:10–12: "Therefore, you kings, be wise; be warned, you rulers of the earth. Serve the LORD with fear and rejoice with trembling. Kiss the Son, lest he be angry and you be destroyed in your way, for his wrath can flare up in a moment. Blessed are all who take refuge in him."

When disasters strike, God wants us to run to Him, not away from Him because we think He is mad at us. No matter what state we find ourselves in, He is there with open arms of love, mercy, and compassion. When disaster strikes, we need only to call upon Him.

GOD IS NOT TO BLAME

We live in a fallen world where disasters and tragedies strike. Rather than blame God for the calamity, we must believe that He can help us handle anything we face. God is not the author of confusion but of love and peace. Jesus brought forth peace to all mankind. All anyone needs to access that peace is to call upon Him. Yet so many blame God. The noise of the culture always gets louder in times of distress.

I live in Birmingham, Alabama, where catastrophic tornadoes swept through the heart of the city April 27, 2011. That day roughly two hundred twisters touched down across the Southeast. Five states reported damage. More than 300 people lost their lives—234 in Alabama alone—and hundreds of buildings were destroyed.[1] As the news media covered the tornado outbreak, I heard more than one person declare, "God is judging our city for its past sins."

Natural disasters tend to bring introspection. This happened both after Hurricane Katrina hit New Orleans, Louisiana, in August 2005 and in March 2011 when an earthquake and tsunami devastated the shore and inland cities of Japan. More than 15,000 people were killed in Japan, and the tsunami set off a nuclear crisis at the Fukushima Daiichi plant.

After the disaster Shintaro Ishihara, the governor of Tokyo, was quoted as saying, "I think [the disaster] is *tembatsu.*" *Tembatsu* means "divine punishment."[2] Ishihara's remarks are similar to those made by then New Orleans Mayor Ray Nagin following Hurricane Katrina. "Surely, God is mad at America," Nagin said. "He sent us hurricane after hurricane after hurricane."[3]

Both men when faced with unspeakable disaster saw the devastation as punishment for human sin. I do believe in divine judgment, but I believe in the awesome love of God even more. The very character of God is love, mercy, and justice, yet what the culture hears about God is often the opposite. After the tsunami in Japan the well-known conservative pundit Glenn Beck said this on his television show: "We can't see the connections here. I'm not saying God is causing earthquakes—well, I'm not not saying that He doesn't either! What God does is God's business. But I'll tell you this...there's a message being sent. And that is, 'Hey, you know that stuff we're doing? Not really working out real well. Maybe we should stop doing some of it.' I'm just saying."[4]

Christian media personalities have also espoused this

outlook. After the earthquake in Haiti that killed more than 200,000 people, one televangelist even declared that God had cursed Haiti. Once again God was depicted as angry and vengeful. Many times, I believe, these honorable leaders have said God must be mad because they lack answers for pain others are walking through. I believe their motives are pure, but what happened to the merciful God of love the Bible talks about?

I love what one preacher told me he said when confronting some ministers who declared the earthquakes that hit Christchurch, New Zealand, in February 2011 to be the judgment of God. The confrontation took place during a gathering of first responders and church leaders who were all meeting to develop a strategy to rescue and help the hurting. As this group of men stood there shouting about God judging Christchurch, my minister-friend rose to his feet and said, "Then God has terrible aim, because many righteous people lost their lives in this great catastrophe!" I agree with this great leader. God was simply the easiest target for those seeking a way to explain the tragedy.

The Bible tells us that the earth is groaning with birth pains (Rom. 8:22), and to me that can describe a planet that is in labor. I do believe that we serve a God who will judge, but He will first show mercy. He wouldn't be God if He didn't have both the power to judge and the power to pardon. The problem is we have allowed the six Ps (parents, peers, politicians, pundits, professors, and preachers) to proclaim God's intentions when it is His Word that really tells us the truth. Romans 11:22 says, "Consider therefore the kindness and sternness of God: sternness to those who fell, but kindness to you, provided that you continue in his kindness."

God has called us to walk in His ways, but that doesn't mean God is judging a city or region whenever disaster strikes. It is easy to pull that card. You can blame God because He doesn't shout down from heaven to defend Himself. We live in a fallen world where tragedy strikes on a daily basis, and it is easy to blame God while ignoring all the good He has done for us. Job 35:9–14 says, "When times get bad, people cry out for help. They cry for relief from being kicked around, but never give God a thought when things go well, when God puts spontaneous songs in their hearts, when God sets out the entire creation as a science classroom, using birds and beasts to teach wisdom. People are arrogantly indifferent to God—until, of course, they're in trouble, and then God is indifferent to them" (THE MESSAGE).

Our temper tantrums, our accusations, our consorting with the embittered—they don't move God. He is moved by our deep desire to simply know Him. We cannot have God on our side if we wander away from His side.

IN GOD WE TRUST?

This nation needs a supernatural awakening to the power of God, His love, and His freedom! How can I say that about a "Christian nation" such as ours, a nation founded on Judeo-Christian values, with a church on every corner, and "In God We Trust" printed on its currency? Maybe it is because the facts are overwhelming.

I believe that if we are not careful, we will reduce God to little more than a mascot. You see, a mascot looks great on bumper stickers and T-shirts, but mascots don't win the games. We like to let people know we're on God's team, but we don't trust Him enough to actually give Him the ball. We declare that God is the Lord of America while, more and more, living like a secular nation. We love God at Christmas and Easter, but we don't want Him to interrupt our daily lives. We honor Him with our lips, but our hearts are far from Him.

I do not believe natural disasters are the result of God's anger toward nations, but I do believe that a nation that seeks God for His protection and mercy will be blessed! Psalm

33:12 says, "Blessed is the nation whose God is the LORD, the people he chose for his inheritance." We must remember that heaven and earth will pass away, but God's words will not pass away (Matt. 24:35). When it comes to judging God's heart and His character, we must rely on God's Word and not on man's opinion!

Chapter 3

GOD IS A GOOD FATHER

I WISH YOU WERE my dad!" I have literally heard that hundreds of times while ministering to students over the last two decades. The exchange usually takes place at an altar area or as I exit the building. During those brief encounters I always feel the same stirring in my heart. I want to wrap my arms around those students and tell them their heavenly Father is a better dad than I am. I want so badly for them to understand the love of God as a father. The problem is many in this generation have no concept of what it means to be loved by a father, and the way a person sees his earthly father most often determines how he will view his heavenly Father.

I love Ephesians 6:4, especially when it's read from THE MESSAGE Bible. It says, "Fathers, don't exasperate your children by coming down hard on them. Take them by the hand and lead them in the way of the Master." What a profound statement to parents—*lead your children in the way of the Master!* The Master is the best example a parent could ever have.

My son, Nate, and I have always been close. Now that he is in college, I reflect on those important early years of his life quite often. We always had a blast together. We loved playing video games and basketball and just having fun together. I

15

was his coach for sports in the early years and then became his
biggest cheerleader when he entered high school and college.

I remember when Nate was just a small boy. We were on
vacation in Florida, and we went for a walk on the beach. We
were holding hands partly because I enjoyed the touch of his
small hand in mine but also because he was rambunctious
and would take off on an adventure if I let him. As we talked,
laughed, and enjoyed the moment, Nate suddenly jumped into
my shadow on the ground and declared, "Look, Dad. I am
walking in your shadow!" It was so surreal for me. I was overwhelmed with responsibility. He is walking in my shadow.

That moment has stuck with me through the years. When
I was not being the best example for whatever reason, I often
would hear Nate's voice in my mind saying, "Look, Dad. I
am walking in your shadow!" His words have been a constant
reminder to me that I have to get this right.

Dads hold a powerful place of influence. More than politicians, professors, or even pastors, dads have an inherent ability
to shape how their children see God. That's because we usually view God in the same way we view our earthly fathers.
This can be tough for someone whose dad was not around to
understand.

When I was very young, my dad was a drug dealer on the
streets of Detroit, Michigan. He worked for the mafia and
had a very hard life. He found Christ when I was five years
old. It really is a miraculous story. No one in our family had
ever really known Christ. My mom got saved first, and shortly
afterward my dad also became a Christian.

After receiving Christ, my dad went off to Bible college in
Colorado. He packed up our family in an old station wagon
and drove away from a life of pain and crime in Detroit. When
my dad finished Bible school, my parents began to pastor
tough little churches in the Deep South. I remember being
around eight years old when our family entered the ministry

full-time. Life was hard for us at times, but in the process our family grew in the deep things of God.

My mom and dad really are my heroes. They both quit high school at a young age only to later finish high school, college, and graduate school. Both of my parents have received master's and doctoral degrees. God completely restored their minds. For years they have been incredible pastors used by God to touch thousands of lives. Many consider them their spiritual parents.

Despite the wonderful, godly lifestyle my parents were now modeling before us kids, it took me a little longer than the others in my family to have a true encounter with God. I was always hungry for God, but I had a tough time believing God loved me for who I was. You see, I was *that* kid—the one who seemed to always find trouble. Then in my teen years it seemed trouble had a way of finding me. My grades were not the best because, really, I had better things to do than study. At least that's what I thought. (Boy, was I wrong!)

I was also the class clown, and while growing up I did some crazy things. I guess you could say I got bored easily. Several years back at my high school reunion so many of my classmates could not believe I had gone into the ministry. As a boy I once burned down an apartment building, and I wrecked a car when I was fourteen. I cooked our family cat in the dryer (total accident), got caught eating the leftover Communion elements after church (not an accident), and almost always had a very smart mouth.

Trust me—I learned early what corporal punishment was all about. *"Wait till your father gets home!"* I must have heard those demonic words come out of my mother's mouth on a daily basis. I would pray the Rapture would happen before my dad got home!

Most of the time I made sure my younger brother was part of my misadventures. I truly believed that no person should go down without an accomplice. The worst thing I remember about being punished was what took place before or after my backside met my father's long skinny black belt. It was the awful "prayer time"! That's right, prayer time. My father felt we needed to pray about my misdeeds before I faced what I usually thought would be the beginning of my new life in eternity. I can remember holding my brother's hand and practically crushing it as my dad forced us to pray for each other before we faced our punishment. Scott, my brother, is a powerful man of God today, but back then he was my partner in crime!

My dad and I have grown very close through the years, but even during those strained teen years I knew he was there for me, and I knew he would listen when I needed an ear. My relationship with my dad has, in many ways, shaped my view of God. I have always viewed God as loving, passionate, bold, holy, powerful, and the embodiment of strength. That actually also describes the way I view my earthly father. Oh, but I left out one characteristic: hard to please. I think all fathers can be demanding at times, but because of my dad's high standards and the way he led our home, I viewed God as a tough disciplinarian you simply never questioned or crossed and maybe as someone waiting for you to mess up.

It took me years to realize I saw God the same way I saw my earthly father. It is a natural progression, if you think about it. It's easy to believe that if our dads have flaws then so must God, and this mistaken perception gets planted in our minds at a young age. This is why believing God is mad at us starts early in life. In later years this thinking can even cause a person to run from God the Father. Someone who had a busy, distant, or demanding father may think it isn't worth trying to please God because He doesn't have time for him or would never accept him. Or someone whose father was a perfectionist might think he just has way too many flaws to be loved.

THE FRUIT OF FATHERLESSNESS

Fathers play the biggest role in shaping our God-view. The Bible uses the word *father* more than 412 times. In the New Testament Jesus referred to God as His Father 107 times. The term *father* best depicts the relationship God wants to have with us. But if this is the case—and it is—then this generation is in a world of hurt. I could tell you literally thousands of stories I have heard while ministering around the nation, stories of abuse and neglect that would sicken you. I praise God that our office has received more than ten thousand testimonies of changed lives, many of which I will share in the coming chapters.

For now, suffice it to say that we have seen firsthand the fruit of fatherless homes. In our home my wife and I know we each play a critical role in raising our children. There is a reason God designed parents to accomplish the monumental task of rearing children together. Yet it seems the traditional view of parenting is under an all-out attack.

In Europe there have even been moves to replace the terms "father" and "mother" on birth certificates in order to accommodate same-sex relationships. Shortly after gay marriage was legalized in Spain, the Official Bulletin of State announced that "the expression 'father' will be replaced with 'Progenitor A,' and 'mother' will be replaced with 'Progenitor B.'" The London *Telegraph* reported that the move "prompted sharp criticism from conservatives and family groups who said language was being rewritten to 'brainwash' the Spanish into accepting a new definition of parenthood."[1]

Europe has been running from traditional values for a long time, but the United States is not far behind them on social issues. After so many years of attacks the very concept of family is now skewed in this generation's eyes. The ideal of a home with both a father and mother leading the way is disappearing. I honestly believe God can bless and guide a home

led by a single parent, but God's perfect plan is for a father
and mother to walk together to guide their children. Sadly it
seems today instead of being the exception, single parenting is
fast becoming the rule.

Here are some astounding statistics: The US Census Bureau
reports that approximately 13.7 million single parents in the
United States are responsible for raising 22 million children,
which is about 26 percent of children under twenty-one years
old.[2] The National Fatherhood Initiative reported that an estimated 24.7 million children (36.3 percent) live absent from
their biological fathers. About 40 percent of the children who
live in fatherless households haven't seen their fathers in at
least a year while 50 percent of the children who don't live
with their fathers have never stepped foot in their father's
home. Roughly 26 percent of absent fathers live in a different
state from their children. One out of every six children is a
stepchild.[3]

Research has shown that about 75 percent of US children
raised in single-parent homes will experience poverty before
the age of eleven while only 20 percent of kids in two-parent
families will experience poverty.[4] The sociological and psycho-
logical effects of not having a dad around are just as alarming.
Sixty-three percent of youth who commit suicide, 85 percent
of all children who exhibit behavioral disorders, and 71 percent of all high school dropouts come from fatherless homes.[5]
Seventy percent of youth in state-operated detention facilities
come from fatherless homes.[6]

Where are the men who will arise and declare as Joshua
did, "But as for me and my household, we will serve the
LORD" (Josh. 24:15)? When the next generation of Israelites
failed to take the same bold stance, look what happened to
Joshua's grandchildren: "After that whole generation had
been gathered to their fathers, another generation grew up,
who knew neither the LORD nor what he had done for Israel"

(Judg. 2:10). I pray this book stirs the priestly representatives to rise up and fill the void.

I am always amazed when I hear parents talk badly of the generation they are raising, as if they had nothing to do with the problems they see. I was at the gym one day working out and praying as usual when God spoke to me, saying, "Son, what parents have hidden from the world their children will someday embarrass them with in public." It is time to turn the lights on in our homes and see what has been crawling around in the dark.

No one is ever ready to be a parent. It takes time to grow into that high calling. I have role models in not only my dad but also in my Savior Jesus Christ, but still I cannot tell you how many times I have failed as a father, how many times I have had to repent to my family for traveling too much in ministry or not being who they really needed me to be. There have been times when I have had to wash my family's feet in repentance. God once said to me, "Son, whomever you wash the feet of you must be willing to die for!" That is exactly what Jesus did with His disciples, and that is exactly the way I feel about my family.

My family has had grace with my flaws, but not everyone has been that blessed. I am so thankful for surrogates who have stepped up many times to play the role of father and mother to those whose parents weren't there for whatever reason. These are the ones who have accepted the call to make a difference in the next generation! There are countless foster parents, adoptive parents, spiritual parents, pastors, coaches, teachers, and advocates who by their actions have deemed the next generation worthy of being loved.

I am reminded of the words of Job, "The fatherless child is snatched from the breast; the infant of the poor is seized for a debt" (Job 24:9). This scripture is very powerful. It declares the state of our nation. This generation has been stolen away by a spirit of fatherlessness, and it has caused us to be very poor. Somewhere along the way the role of dad has been diminished. On television sitcoms most dads are depicted as mindless, aloof, arrogant, or disinterested in their families' daily lives. So with Hollywood making dads look like bumps on a log and so many absent fathers in our nation, how in the world can someone who has been robbed of a father see God correctly?

PAINTING A TRUE PICTURE OF THE FATHER

Throughout Scripture we read that God is our Father, so it is easy for us to think He is like our earthly father. It's easy for us to think, "Maybe God is just mad at me!" I wonder how many people reading this book wish they had heard the words I used to dread, "Wait till your father gets home!" So many in this generation have never seen their dads walk through the front door; when they hear people say, "God is your Father," they wince at the thought. In fact, it may scare them or simply sound like Greek to them. We say things such as, "Let's worship the Father in heaven," and they think, "Why?"

I am reminded of one particular night in the summer of 2010. While ministering at a youth camp in Florida, I was caught off guard during the altar experience. Hundreds of students were weeping for more of God, and I was sitting on the edge of the stage just enjoying the encounter taking place and not realizing I was about to be shaken to my core.

"Will you wrestle with us?" Those were the words I heard from four very large African American guys from Miami. I'm not kidding when I say these guys were huge, and they were standing right in front of me. I said, "You guys are crazy! You don't want any of this!" We all laughed at the very awkward moment. You see, they were responding to the altar experience that night. During my message to the hundreds of students I had talked about the deep relationship I have with my son and daughter. I had shared how I love to dance with my little daughter and wrestle with my son. These four strapping young men were asking a very real question.

After we laughed for a moment, the laughter turned to tears running down their faces. Then they said, "If you won't wrestle with us, then will you hold us? Sir, you see, we have never been hugged by a dad." I went to my knees and wrapped those four guys up for probably thirty minutes. I remember returning to my hotel room late that night and sitting on the side of the bed weeping. My shirt was covered with tears that did not belong to me.

The tears that now stained my shirt were from these young men. These were tears that belonged on the shirts of dads who simply never showed up to be fathers. These guys had never experienced a simple hug. The church is very good at telling people, "Your heavenly Father loves you!" But we don't always realize how many people just don't understand that. When we say, "God is your Father," "God wants you to be His child," "God has plans for His children," a very large portion of this generation has a skewed view of what that actually means.

Solomon, the wisest man who ever lived, declared the importance of mom and dad: "Listen with respect to the father who raised you, and when your mother grows old, don't neglect her. Buy truth—don't sell it for love or money; buy wisdom, buy education, buy insight. Parents rejoice when their children turn out well; wise children become proud parents. So make your father happy! Make your mother proud!" (Prov. 23:22–25, The Message).

I have rarely met a young man who doesn't think his mother is a saint, but I have met many who have nothing to say about their dads. How do you tell a teenager with no dad how to view God? This is the dilemma of this generation: no dad, no understanding of God.

Early one morning I heard my son yell for me from his bedroom. Nate was about six years old at the time. I looked at the clock, and it was past 2:00 a.m. I jumped out of bed and ran into his bedroom fearing the worst. I asked Nate what was wrong. He said, "Daddy, I just needed to know that you were home." I said, "What? Why would you say that? Of course I am home."

He said, "Daddy you have been gone so much I just needed to know you were home." I remember crawling into bed with him and holding him close to me. It was one of many wake-up calls I have had as a father. Since that time I have said the same thing to God: "Dad, I just need to know You're here with me!" I believe God loves it when we talk to Him like that.

For all the reasons we have discussed so far in this chapter, it is imperative that I address what makes God a good Father. If you realize who God is as a Father, you will never again feel alone! This is so important I am going to spend Part Two giving ten attributes and actions of God. I believe knowing these truths will help address all or at least many of your questions about God's role as our Father. Maybe if we see God for who He really is, then it will allow us to understand that He isn't mad at us. Get ready. Your journey is expanding.

PART 2

GETTING TO KNOW THE FATHER

Chapter 4

GOD ADOPTED US INTO HIS FAMILY

E PHESIANS 1 REVEALS something about God that is critical for us to understand if we are to truly get the revelation that He is not mad at us. In verses 4–6 we read, "For he chose us in him before the creation of the world to be holy and blameless in his sight. In love he predestined us to be adopted as his sons through Jesus Christ, in accordance with his pleasure and will—to the praise of his glorious grace, which he has freely given us in the One he loves."

Did you catch the key word in that verse? God *chose* us to be adopted into His family long before we were born. We are His children—not His stepchildren or grandchildren, but His *children*. When we accept Christ as our Savior, we become part of God's family. With our adoption comes God's total acceptance of us. He accepts us into His family just as we are.

The truth that God accepts us could set so many people free if they would just believe it. I have seen the pain in the eyes of so many people who long to just be accepted. I remember standing in front of thousands of students at a conference in New Zealand. They were gathered around the platform worshipping God. As I leaned out over the platform, I noticed several teenage girls with their hands lifted in worship. What was shocking to me was that there were cut marks up and down their arms. I leaned over and spoke to the girls in a whisper. I said, "Why are you cutting yourselves when He has already been cut for you?"

The young ladies began to weep as God did an awesome work in their lives. We have seen God heal these kinds of deep emotional wounds again and again in our evangelistic meetings. In fact, in many of our services students and adults who cut themselves see their physical scars disappear during or immediately after the service! I believe with all of my heart that cutting is directly tied to an inner anger, hurt, and pain that is only temporarily relieved by the pain released when the person cuts his or her body. It is hard to explain if you've never experienced that kind of hurt. Someone very close to me once told me he cut himself because it allowed him to see proof of the pain he felt on the inside.

True freedom and healing of these deep hurts will come to this generation only when they realize the Father has adopted them and accepts them completely. I believe God is calling many in the body of Christ to help this generation overcome their past so He can take control of their future. Seeds planted in our youth will eventually yield fruit according to their kind. That's why we must help dig up the bad roots and replace them with fresh seeds of God's love.

I know this kind of healing is possible because I've seen it happening all around the country. I remember a fourteen-year-old from Alabama, who sent us a powerful testimony, saying, "I started cutting myself because I thought God was mad at me after my grandmother was taken from me. But I realized God was mad for me. I love Him!"

Another young person sent me this message after I spoke at an incredible youth movement in Hamilton, Alabama, called The Ramp. She wasn't even there but had watched the service via live stream on the Internet. "I know you have never met me," she wrote, "but I was watching you online when you were at The Ramp. I'm twenty-one, and I have cut myself for years! Life just got too hard to deal with after losing my mom and my fiancé. I had intense scars all over from cutting, and all but one is gone. I just wanted to let you know that."

This young woman was just watching a church service online and God healed her! I love testimonies like that. Freedom from the pain of our pasts comes only through our adoption as God's children.

Our Little Gift From Heaven

I am so blessed to have the most gorgeous daughter in the whole world. On January 10, 2003, my beautiful daughter, Abigail XiuHe Schatzline, was born somewhere near Nanchang, China. According to her orphanage she was found fifteen days after she was born in a park where her biological mother had left her. China has a "one-child" policy that forbids certain classes of people from having more than one child.

Abby spent the first nine months of her life in a Christian orphanage. In October 2003, after more than two years of preparation and mountains of paperwork, Karen, Nate, and I traveled to China to pick up our little angel. Adopting Abby was our single greatest accomplishment as a family.

The first nine months of Abby's life are a mystery for the most part because she is too young to remember those early days. And because of the language barrier, we were not able to get much information about her background from the orphanage. But you know what? Despite the way Abby's life started, she now has a family. She has a home. She is our little gift from heaven, and we believe God has amazing plans for her. Abby is far from abandoned, illegitimate, or unwanted— and as God's child, so are you.

At the orphanage Abby was given the name XiuHe, which we were told means "lotus flower" in Chinese. We were told that when she was found in the park, she was lying next to a lotus flower, so that became her name. When we adopted our little girl we gave her a new name, Abigail, because it means "my father's joy," but we kept XiuHe as her middle name. You see, when a father rescues you, he doesn't leave you where you were found; he has the power to take you with him past that place. That's what happened with Abby. Her name is a constant reminder that she is no longer alone next to the lotus flower—she is her father's joy!

The Bible tells us the Father will never leave us as orphans. John 14:15–18 says, "If you love me, you will obey what I command. And I will ask the Father, and he will give you another Counselor to be with you forever—the Spirit of truth. The world cannot accept him, because it neither sees him nor knows him. But you know him, for he lives with you and will be in you. I will not leave you as orphans; I will come to you." *Boom*—there it is! Jesus declared that even after He was gone from the earth He would ask the Father to give someone to fight for you.

Who is that person? The Holy Spirit! In the passage above, Jesus was telling the world that we have a Dad and we will never be orphaned. Even when Jesus was no longer physically present, He would never leave us all alone. That is amazing love! He said in His Word, "I love you so much that you will always have a Dad to call out to!"

Romans 8:15 says, "The Spirit you received does not make you slaves, so that you live in fear again; rather, the Spirit you received brought about your adoption to sonship, and by him we cry, 'Abba Father'" (niv, 2011). We are God's sons and daughters, and we can call Him our Father. At any time, under any circumstances, we can cry out to Him, "Dad!" and He will answer. What an awesome Father!

Chapter 5

GOD IS NOT AN ABSENTEE FATHER

A LTHOUGH GOD IS a loving Father who promises to never abandon us, there are times in our walk with God when we feel all alone. I love what Denise Frangipane wrote in her booklet *Overcoming Fear*: "Our first place of victory is in believing the truth concerning our relationship with God."[1] Victory—over fear or anything else—comes when we realize God wants to be in relationship with us. That is Christianity 101, but I believe many believers missed that course in the early part of their walk!

Despair and loneliness can overwhelm even the strongest of Christians. I once heard it said that God whispers in the good times and shouts in the bad. Wouldn't it be so much easier if we could go back and walk in the cool of the evening with Him as Adam did, or if we could have a burning bush experience as Moses did? I have often said my greatest goal when I get to heaven is not to see loved ones who died before me, dive headfirst into the River of Life, or dance on the streets made of gold and fine jewels, but rather to run and find Jesus. I want to go for a walk with Him. I want to thank Him for being my Savior and Friend.

What I am sharing is so hard for a person who has been abandoned by a parent to understand. It's hard for a person whose father was never there to believe God the

Father enjoys spending time with him and is watching over him. But God's Word is true no matter what we have been through. Psalm 46:1 tells us, "God is a safe place to hide, ready to help when we need him" (THE MESSAGE). God's door is always open to us no matter what we are walking through, and He provides rest.

We have been given another awesome promise in Matthew 11:28–30: "Are you tired? Worn out? Burned out on religion? Come to me. Get away with me and you'll recover your life. I'll show you how to take a real rest. Walk with me and work with me—watch how I do it. Learn the unforced rhythms of grace. I won't lay anything heavy or ill-fitting on you. Keep company with me and you'll learn to live freely and lightly" (THE MESSAGE). The last part of that passage says it best: "*Keep company with me!*" In other words, God is saying, "Let's hang out!"

We have all gone through seasons when it seems the heavens were silent. A dear friend and mentor of mine named Glen Berteau was ministering to me one day while I was walking through a very quiet and lonely season. I needed a word from God, and it just seemed that the heavens were silent. He said, "Pat, the teacher never talks when he gives a test."[2] Those words brought life to me. God had not gone anywhere; He was just walking me through a season of testing. I have learned that nothing can be trusted until it is tested!

The psalmist described how much God loves us in Psalm 139: "Even from a distance, you know what I'm thinking. You know when I leave and when I get back; I'm never out of your sight. You know everything I'm going to say before I start the first sentence. I look behind me and you're there, then up ahead and you're there, too—your reassuring presence, coming and going. This is too much, too wonderful—I can't take it all in!" (vv. 1–6, THE MESSAGE). That passage truly describes the Father. I wish I could read this verse to every person who has ever felt abandoned. As the psalmist said, "God's love is just too wonderful. I can't take it all in!"

I can still remember hearing the curse words that were pouring out of the thirteen-year-old football player's mouth as he stood over the young quarterback he had just tackled. The quarterback was screaming in pain, but that didn't seem to bother Jimmy, who played on a football team I helped coach. A few minutes before, I had sent the team out on the field in the fourth quarter to try and stage a defensive stop to win the game. But when Jimmy suddenly noticed that no one was in the stands to watch him play, he became upset and then out of control.

Just before the play he screamed from the field, "Coach, where is my mom?" I didn't have any answers for him. I just yelled back, "I am not sure; just get your head in the game." He screamed back at me, "She promised she would be here!" I said, "Jimmy, just get your head in the game!" It was what any coach would yell, but I didn't realize how upset Jimmy was that no one had come to see him play.

When the referee blew the whistle, Jimmy ran as hard as he could and sacked the quarterback with such force he broke the young man's collarbone. Then he just stood over him cursing and screaming, "That is for no one coming to watch me play!" That day I stood back and thought about all of the broken promises that had led to this eruption of pain.

GOD KEEPS HIS WORD

Abandonment, broken promises, and a lost sense of belonging are running rampant. Young people are screaming for a Father who keeps His word. The good news is that God always keeps His promises! It doesn't matter who you are or where you are from—this promise hasn't changed. Deuteronomy 7:7–8 says, "God wasn't attracted to you and didn't choose you because you were big and important—the fact is, there was almost nothing to you. He did it out of sheer love, keeping the promise he made to your ancestors" (THE MESSAGE). God *always* keeps His promises!

Through Jesus our lives are complete. That is called walking in covenant. A covenant is a promise. Second Corinthians 1:20–22 explains the covenant we enter into when we accept Christ: "Whatever God has promised gets stamped with the Yes of Jesus. In him, this is what we preach and pray, the great Amen, God's Yes and our yes together, gloriously evident. God affirms us, making us a sure thing in Christ, putting his Yes within us. By his Spirit he has stamped us with his eternal pledge—a sure beginning of what he is destined to complete" (THE MESSAGE).

I have learned that the thing that makes you the angriest is the thing you are most likely called to help conquer. I think after years of speaking to students and adults, what makes me the most annoyed is when people cannot receive the love of the Father because they've been given the wrong image of God. I believe Psalm 88:1–4 describes the pain in many people's hearts: "God, you're my last chance of the day. I spend the night on my knees before you. Put me on your salvation agenda; take notes on the trouble I'm in. I've had my fill of trouble; I'm camped on the edge of hell. I'm written off as a lost cause, one more statistic, a hopeless case" (THE MESSAGE). I've met so many people who feel written off as a lost cause!

Periodically when I talk about the love of the Father at youth conferences, I will illustrate His love by bringing a young lady on stage and dancing with her. The dance is always very proper and pure. It all started at home with my daughter, Abby. She is a hopeless romantic who believes at this stage that Daddy is her prince. She loves it when I slow down long enough to simply dance with her. She will turn on the iPod to one of her favorite songs and say, "Daddy, would you take time to dance with me?"

Honestly, sometimes I get so busy I forget what a big deal

this is to our relationship. But when I hear her sweet voice making that simple request, I will stop and pick her up, and we will dance around the room. Inevitably I end up in tears as I hold my little gift. I realize the day will come when times like these will be few and far between, so I cherish every moment with my little girl. And I know she's not the only little girl who wants to dance with her father.

On one particular night while I was speaking at a large youth conference in Ohio with hundreds of students gathered around the altar, I began to tell the crowd who God the Father truly can be in their lives. I'd asked the students to raise their hands if they had never felt the love of a father or had grown up without their dad around. I watched as one young lady raised her hand and began to weep uncontrollably at the fact that she had no dad around. I asked her to come up on the stage, and I danced with her for just a few moments to demonstrate the love of a father. A few days later she sent me a message on Facebook:

> Hey, I'm that girl from the conference, and you told me that God said I was beautiful and stuff and you danced with me…Haha! Yeah, I'm her, and what you told me God said, well, that completely changed the way I look at things now. I used to call myself ugly all the time, but now I do look at myself as being pretty, and I can bet you changed a lot of people's lives that night. I know you changed mine, and you did it for the best. Thank you so much. There is a reason God wanted me to be there…♥ Thank you so much.

That is just one of hundreds of testimonies I receive from students who come to realize that the love of God is real and tangible. Those who have been hurt and abandoned often see God as the Father who isn't a father, or they may see God as someone who doesn't keep His word. Yet God the Father has His eyes upon each of us. He is watching our every move with excitement and compassion. I want everyone reading this book to know that He sees your future, He knows the purpose for your life, and He is proud of you. He likes what He made, and He wants you to know He will not abandon you!

GOD IS ALWAYS THERE

There is not a child out there who hasn't been afraid at night or who hasn't gotten scared because he was lost and thought he had been abandoned. Thousands of kids go to bed at night wishing they could hear the door of their house open and someone say, "Dad's home!"

Psalm 139:7–12 asks, "Is there anyplace I can go to avoid your Spirit? to be out of your sight? If I climb to the sky, you're there! If I go underground, you're there! If I flew on morning's wings to the far western horizon, you'd find me in a minute— you're already there waiting! Then I said to myself, 'Oh, he even sees me in the dark! At night I'm immersed in the light!' It's a fact: darkness isn't dark to you; night and day, darkness and light, they're all the same to you" (THE MESSAGE).

God is always there. He is your night-light on the darkest of nights. He won't run out on you. You are the object of His affection, and He isn't going to suddenly decide to find a new one. Last summer I heard the same statement two weeks in a row while traveling in Texas and Arizona: "Pat, my dad used to do what you do. He was a preacher, but then he decided to go find a new family!" My heart ached for these two teens. Their dads had left town, found new families, and abandoned them and their call. And now these teenagers were left to figure out why.

My mom never really knew her biological father. Her dad, a man I have met only once, got my grandmother pregnant just before he went off to fight in the Korean War. They were not married when he went away to fight, and he was later a prisoner of war for a long period of time. There was no contact from him, and he eventually was listed as missing in action. Fearing the worst, my grandmother moved on with her life now raising a little girl. She later married a man I always considered to be my grandfather.

My mom's biological father was released from captivity after the war ended and came home to find out my grandmother had married. Still, my mom's biological father tried to stay in touch with her. He would call her or write periodically, but time and life got in the way. He made her a great deal of promises, such as that he would call her on her sixteenth birthday, but he never made the call. He wasn't good at keeping promises.

This hurt my mom deeply and made her feel somewhat abandoned. Later in life this would cause her to feel that God wouldn't keep His promises, and it caused her to struggle to see God as her Father. It took her years to realize that God isn't like her earthly dad. He actually keeps His promises. It wasn't until she was able to separate God the Father from the father who wasn't there that she found freedom.

You Are Always on God's Mind

God always has you on His mind. Did you know that Jesus prays for you? Hebrews 7:25 says, "Therefore he is able to save completely those who come to God through him, because *he always lives to intercede for them*" (emphasis added). Then we read in Psalm 42:7–8, "Chaos calls to chaos, to the tune of whitewater rapids. Your breaking surf, your thundering breakers crash and crush me. Then GOD promises to love me all day, sing songs all through the night! *My life is God's prayer*" (THE MESSAGE, emphasis added).

God the Father is there for you. He sings songs through your darkest night, just as the psalmist says, and your life is His prayer! When you get to heaven and get a chance to ask

God what He prays about, do you know what He will say? *You!* You're His prayer life!

Last year I was speaking at a men's conference in Canada. During one of the services I spoke about the Father's love. That night a gentleman in his eighties came up to me at the end of the service weeping. He told me that when he was a boy, his father went off to war. He told me how he and his dad had walked to the train station in the snow the day his father left. He watched as his father boarded the train, and then his dad yelled to him that he would return.

His father was killed in action and never came home. That happened decades ago, but the elderly man told me he had not cried since the day his dad left for war. He had spent his whole life angry with his father for never coming home, but that night God healed his hurt as he realized the depth of the Father's love. He said as he prayed, God took him back to that day and showed him that Jesus was right there with him as his dad left. He was never alone. This precious man had finally realized the love of his heavenly Father and allowed the truth of who God is replace what he had come to believe. The same revelation this man received is true for you as well—God will never abandon you!

Chapter 6

GOD MAKES US SECURE

PSALM 16:5 SAYS, "LORD, you have assigned me my portion and my cup; you have made my lot secure." As a dad I play many important roles, but I believe my highest responsibility is to provide safety and security to my family. If we hear a noise at night, I would never ask my wife to go check to see if there is an intruder. I would never yell for my kids to see what all the commotion is about. No! I would bolt out of the bed ready to defend my home, and I have done just that. Why? Because that is my role as a husband and dad.

The security I must provide is not just to protect my family from harm but also to help them feel secure in themselves as individuals. There have been times when I could feel the insecurity in our home. Many times I had caused it because I was not walking in wisdom. Driven by success, I often put my family on the back burner to chase my dreams. I was ruled by my emotions, looking for security in ministry, and many times I was very difficult to live with. My wife, Karen, is the one who often helped me realize that I was being overcome by insecurity and that it was affecting the atmosphere in our home. I thank God that through her love and gentleness, Karen helped me return to a place of feeling secure in who I am as a man and the leader of my home.

When my son, Nate, has faced times of fear and doubt, I

have always been able to help him know that everything is
going to be OK. Whether he was preparing for a test at school,
earning a spot on a team, or going on his first date, I did my
best to steady his emotions. The same is true of Abby, but I
learned quickly that girls are very different from boys. You
can pull a boy out of insecurity by championing his gifts or
accomplishments, or by coaching him to the next level. I have
found that little girls gain security when someone—namely
their dad—takes the time to remind them how special they
are or simply listen to them.

I remember one particular day when Abby came home
from school looking as though she had not had the best day. I
asked Abby how her day at school went. There are not many
Asian Americans where we live, so Abby stands out among
her peers. Abby is loved and very popular at school. Many of
the kids think it is their job to protect her because she is the
smallest in her class. Nevertheless, kids sometimes ask the
dumbest questions, especially when it comes to race or color.
Abby has been asked things such as, "Do you eat rice for every
meal?" or "Why does your mommy not look like you?"

Most of the time she handles these questions as a real
champion, but other times we can tell it gets to her. That day
when I asked about her day, she looked very distant. When
I probed further and asked her what was wrong, she said,
"Daddy, am I ugly?" In an instant I picked her up and sat her
up high in front of me and said, "Sweetheart, never use those
words again. You are the most beautiful little girl I have ever
seen. You're beautiful inside and out!" Her mood, her mind-
set, and her demeanor instantly changed. I told her, "Don't
you ever doubt how pretty you are! God created His very best
when He made you." She has never uttered those words again.
Why? Because her father made her feel secure!

God has called all of us to walk in the security of His love.
Your greatness is not something you possess on your own. Your
greatness is in the fact that God has chosen to put His Spirit

in you because you are His child. God gave us this promise in Galatians 3:26–29: "You are all sons of God through faith in Christ Jesus, for all of you who were baptized into Christ have clothed yourselves with Christ. There is neither Jew nor Greek, slave nor free, male nor female, for you are all one in Christ Jesus. If you belong to Christ, then you are Abraham's seed, and heirs according to the promise." This promise wasn't just for the church of the first century—it's for us too!

You Don't Have to Feel Insecure

Have you ever met someone who looks like he is wearing a neon sign that says, "Do you like me?" The most dangerous person to the body of Christ is not the one who is lethargic or walks in fear or knowingly teaches false doctrine. The most dangerous person to the body of Christ is the insecure person. Why? Because insecure people can easily be swayed in any direction the wind is blowing. They can easily forget the Father's love when they are presented with something that will give them an emotional high.

God is looking for those who will stand firm in what they believe. James 1:6–8 says, "But when he asks, he must believe and not doubt, because he who doubts is like a wave of the sea, blown and tossed by the wind. That man should not think he will receive anything from the Lord; he is a double-minded man, unstable in all he does."

Insecure people are double-minded, and whether they realize it or not, their actions often deny the love of God. Insecurity is a neon sign that says, "My God is not big enough to handle my situation!" It is caused by fear of what others think and by believing the flesh over the Holy Spirit. In essence, insecurity is a form of pride—and pride is one thing God hates! God hates pride because He loves people, and pride prevents people from receiving help from God.

There are two forces that are always at war within us. The

battle is between the flesh and the spirit. This battle is so intense the apostle Paul spent Romans chapters 5 through 8 describing it. He wrote in Romans 7:21–25, "So I find this law at work: When I want to do good, evil is right there with me. For in my inner being I delight in God's law; but I see another law at work in the members of my body, waging war against the law of my mind and making me a prisoner of the law of sin at work within my members. What a wretched man I am! Who will rescue me from this body of death? Thanks be to God—through Jesus Christ our Lord! So then, I myself in my mind am a slave to God's law, but in the sinful nature a slave to the law of sin."

The flesh can control our attitude, desires, and victories if we don't set boundaries based on God's Word to govern our thoughts and actions. Romans 8:5–8 says, "Those who live according to the sinful nature have their minds set on what that nature desires; but those who live in accordance with the Spirit have their minds set on what the Spirit desires. The mind of sinful man is death, but the mind controlled by the Spirit is life and peace; the sinful mind is hostile to God. It does not submit to God's law, nor can it do so. Those controlled by the sinful nature cannot please God."

Ultimately insecurity comes from a root of rejection. Somewhere along the way, the insecure person felt he was not good enough or he felt abandoned. This root of rejection will cause a person to think God won't always protect him. He feels like the writer of Psalm 30:6–7 did, "When I felt secure, I said, 'I will never be shaken.' O Lord, when you favored me, you made my mountain stand firm; but when you hid your face, I was dismayed."

The psalmist is describing someone who is secure when he feels God's presence and insecure when he doesn't feel Him. God expects us to push past our feelings no matter what we face! During a trying period in my life the Lord told me that if I would maintain my integrity in the tough times, He would give me a greater level of spiritual authority in the good times. I had to learn to trust that God is always in control no matter how I feel. I found that I would begin to lose my ability to see myself correctly if I started listening to the voice of the flesh instead of learning who God had called me to be.

Has anyone ever spoken to you in a way that made you feel like less of a person? This can cause some of the deepest insecurities. Those negative words spoken to you can cause you to hurt so bad you begin to doubt who you are as a person. Words can destroy a person. The tongue can be a lethal weapon. Proverbs 18:21 says, "The tongue has the power of life and death, and those who love it will eat its fruit."

Maybe others' actions caused you to feel rejected. They didn't keep their promises, they walked all over your feelings, or they walked away from you. When this happened, you began to question your value. Circumstances determine your stance. Psalm 112:7–8 says, "He will have no fear of bad news; his heart is steadfast, trusting in the LORD. His heart is secure, he will have no fear; in the end he will look in triumph on his foes." God is saying through this verse, "I have given you the victory over all of your circumstances— regardless of who is against you!"

What you must realize is that many times God will move people out of your life in order to protect you. At the time they may make it seem as if you were not worthy of them, but really God allowed them to leave your life for a reason. Sometimes rejection is protection. You have to trust that God always has your best interests in mind. The battle within us tends to manifest as a war with other people. James says it so well: "What causes fights and quarrels among you? Don't they come from your desires that battle within you?" (James 4:1). The victory comes when we begin to realize not just who we are but who is in us.

YOU ARE WHO GOD SAYS YOU ARE

The apostle Paul was a brilliant apologist and scholar. Yet his confidence was not in his intellect or preaching ability. He wrote in 1 Corinthians 2:1–5: "When I came to you, brothers, I did not come with eloquence or superior wisdom as I proclaimed to you the testimony about God. For I resolved to know nothing while I was with you except Jesus Christ and him crucified. I came to you in weakness and fear, and with much trembling. My message and my preaching were not with wise and persuasive words, but with a demonstration of the Spirit's power, so that your faith might not rest on men's wisdom, but on God's power."

Your faith cannot rest on man's opinion. You do not need others' approval to be who God called you to be. You just have to realize that your Father has declared that you are His! God protects what He purchases. In the powerful passage above Paul was declaring that he knew who he was and who had sent him.

For many years I battled deep insecurity. It controlled me at almost every level. What others thought of me controlled every aspect of my life. One of the most powerful scriptures I have ever read is 1 Corinthians 1:26–28: "Take a good look, friends, at who you were when you got called into this life. I don't see many of 'the brightest and the best' among you, not many influential, not many from high-society families. Isn't it obvious that God deliberately chose men and women that the culture overlooks and exploits and abuses, chose these 'nobodies' to expose the hollow pretensions of the 'somebodies'?" (THE MESSAGE). When this verse really came alive in my heart, I realize that God can use anyone. In fact, I think He enjoys using the ones who are the least "qualified" to be in front of the world as His representatives!

During my first ten years of ministry, whenever I finished speaking publicly I felt like a complete failure. My favorite meal after a church service was a plate of self-pity and a glass of fear! I will never forget when I was finally able to get free from deep insecurity. It happened to be in Toronto, Ontario, where I was speaking at a conference. On this particular occasion all of the forces of insecurity intersected. The conference was canceled due to bad weather, and I was stuck in a hotel near the Toronto airport. To make matters worse, my wife and son were at home hundreds of miles away, and Nate was battling ear infections so severe one of his eardrums burst.

Nate had screamed over the phone, "Daddy, please come home!" I felt like the worst dad in the world. He needed me to be there with him, but I was stuck in a hotel. I remember crying out to God for over seven hours. I was so burned out from fear and insecurity I was ready to quit the ministry. As I wrestled with God in prayer, I heard Him speak something so rich to me. He said, "Pat, you have never resurrected; you only continue to redecorate the tomb! Pat, you have to get free before you try to free others."

God needed to rip out of me years of insecurity and a spirit of failure that seemed to have always been a part of my life. I'd spent years worrying about what others thought of me and being less than who I was called to be. These are things I needed to confront but never had the courage to deal with. I thank God that He cares enough about us to put us in a place of confrontation. I have always said the greatest thing that can happen is for a person to get stuck by himself in a room with God, because that's where God will confront the issues in his life.

In that hotel room God showed me what it truly meant to be resurrected in Him. He said, "Pat, remember when Jesus came out of the tomb? Mary thought He was the gardener." He then took me to that story in Scripture, which is found in John 20:15. God continued to speak to me and said, "Pat, she didn't get it wrong! Jesus *is* the gardener. In Genesis 2 Adam was the gardener of Eden. Jesus is the second Adam. So in other words, when Jesus came out of the tomb of death, He became the Second Adam."

When you finally get free of your past, and when you finally resurrect after the death of your history and pain, you will arise to your original purpose. Mary didn't make a mistake when she said, "You must be the gardener." She was declaring that Jesus was now the Second Adam. The first Adam brought death to mankind through his disobedience, but Jesus, the Second Adam, willingly sacrificed His life and through His death brought life to us all (Rom. 5:12–19).

When you are resurrected in Christ, you now represent someone free of your history. You represent someone who knows she is completely forgiven, accepted, and loved by God. You are secure in Christ! Ephesians 2:1–6 says, "It wasn't so long ago that you were mired in that old stagnant life of sin. You let the world, which doesn't know the first thing about living, tell you how to live. You filled your lungs with polluted unbelief, and then exhaled disobedience. We all did it, all of us doing what we felt like doing, when we felt like doing it, all of us in the same boat. It's a wonder God didn't lose his temper and do away with the whole lot of us. Instead, immense in mercy and with an incredible love, he embraced us. He took our sin-dead lives and made us alive in Christ. He did all this on his own, with no help from us! Then he picked us up and set us down in highest heaven in company with Jesus, our Messiah" (THE MESSAGE).

Since that day I have done my very best to never let that spirit of despair bring me down. Oh, it has tried to sneak back in, but I know I am more than a conqueror through Christ (Rom. 8:37). Your freedom, like mine, is totally dependent on Christ.

I will close this section by talking about my best friend, my beautiful wife, Karen. God truly blessed me when He brought her into my life. Karen represents to me God's purity on loan. I have seen God use her to change thousands of lives as she ministers His love. Most of all she has changed my view of God! She has taught me to trust God. Karen wasn't raised in ministry like me, and that has proved invaluable. She didn't develop the distrust that comes from seeing too many negative church issues.

I have said for years that the Trinity was in the Garden of Eden. The inhabitants were God the Father, the Son as represented by Adam, and the Holy Spirit as represented by Eve. Karen represents Eve in our home; she represents the Holy Spirit. She has the power to recognize the enemy just as Eve recognized the devil as a serpent sent to destroy. Remember in Genesis 3 when God showed up in the Garden of Eden looking for Adam and Eve after their devastating fall into sin? God asked them who had caused the fall. Eve immediately said it was the devil, and God said, "You are right, and there will be war between the two of you." (See verse 15.) Eve had the power to recognize the enemy, and so does my Eve!

God uses Karen to awaken me to so much. I have learned over the years that I had better listen to her. She carries a wisdom that has rescued us so many times. The Bible says in Ephesians 5:28, "In this same way, husbands ought to love their wives as their own bodies. He who loves his wife loves himself."

I realized that in order to protect my gift from God, I had better begin to like who I am. I have learned that I cannot truly love my wife unless I love myself. It took me a while to learn this, but when I did, it changed our marriage. When I became secure in who God called me to be, our home became a place of refuge and power. My own security allowed me to bring a new level of leadership to my family. I can pray over our home, guard what we do, and declare who we are when I am secure.

I challenge every leader to realize that you are the representative of God in your home. I have asked myself many times in prayer, "Do I want to be pastored by me?" Trust me,

I didn't always have a positive answer to that question. I have had to change in order to assure the very future of my home. But it is exhilarating when the results of your hard work to be secure show up in your children. I have learned that if I am secure, then my wife is secure, and my children represent a home led well.

Do you see how awesome God is? When I learned to trust God to be the source of my security, not only did my life change, but also so did that of my wife, my children, and so many others God has called me to reach. As you accept the truth about God and the security you'll find in Him, your life will change too.

Chapter 7

GOD ALLOWS US TO CHOOSE

A COUPLE YEARS AGO I found that I was way out of shape. I had not taken care of my body, and a doctor's report let me know I had better make some changes. I decided to begin to jog every day as a way of getting healthy. It was one of the best decisions I have ever made. Running every morning not only benefited me physically, but it also helped me spiritually. During those jogs I am able to get alone with God and talk with my Savior. Now instead of drudgery my morning run is one of my favorite times of the day.

After my workout I am usually pretty thirsty. Sometimes I feel I could drink a gallon of water, but I've learned something in the years God has blessed me to walk the earth. That glass of cool, refreshing water won't come and get me—I have to go get it. I can't expect anyone to just bring it to me either. If I want something to drink, I have to take the initiative.

The same is true spiritually. If you're thirsty for God, there is only one way it can be quenched. Jesus said in John 7:37, "If anyone is thirsty, let him come to me and drink." That is the key. Anyone who is thirsty for more of God must *choose* to come to Him and drink of the living water. Revelation 22:17 tells us the water is free, but we still must choose to drink it!

My parents are Christians, and I was raised in church from the age of five, but I had to choose to follow Christ. I heard

Him call out to me when I was sixteen years old, and I chose
to follow Him. Have I been a perfect Christian? No! Have
I fallen down at times? Yes! But His love for me has never
wavered.

I know many people wonder how a loving God could allow
anyone to go to hell. The reason is that God gave us the power
to choose. And if a person decides to not follow Christ, God
cannot rescue him from the consequences of that choice. God
loves us enough to pursue us and knock on the door of our
hearts, but He also allows us to choose whether we will follow
Him. He isn't a bully!

Did you know that God chose us before we ever had a
chance to choose Him? How? I am reminded of a conversation I had with my daughter one day when I was taking her
to school. Abby is not a morning person, so our drives to
school have to be animated to get her good and awake. It is a
process, but after a while we'll end up singing, playing games,
or having tickling sessions all while I'm navigating through
traffic. One morning as I was reaching into the backseat to
tickle her, she suddenly said, "Daddy, can I ask you something?" I said, "Sure, sweetheart, what is it?" She said, "How
did you love me before you ever met me?"

I was frozen for a moment trying to understand exactly
what she was asking. I asked, "What do you mean, Abby?"
She said, "Well, Daddy, you always tell me that you and
Mommy loved me before you ever met me. How did you do
that?"

My answer for her was simple. I said, "Abby, I can't explain
it, except to say it is a lot like the way Jesus loved us before
we loved and met Him. Sweetheart, we just had a love for
you before we ever met you. Then God brought you into our
lives to be in our family!" God knew that at conception Abby
would need us and, more than that, we would need her. Abby
was sent to fill a void that only she could fill.

The same is true of us. Before we ever met Him, Jesus was

madly in love with us and wanted us to be part of His family. John 1:12 says, "Yet to all who received him, to those who believed in his name, he gave the right to become children of God." When you accept Christ as your Savior, you are no longer illegitimate, abandoned, or an orphan. Instead you are a part of an awesome family. But the key is that you have to accept Christ. You must choose!

The Bible says in Romans 10:9, "If you confess with your mouth, 'Jesus is Lord,' and believe in your heart that God raised him from the dead, you will be saved." It is that easy! But God will not force you to love Him. He loves us first so that we can love Him last! That means there is no going back. Take a look at 1 John 1:8–10: "If we claim that we're free of sin, we're only fooling ourselves. A claim like that is errant nonsense. On the other hand, if we admit our sins—make a clean breast of them—he won't let us down; he'll be true to himself. He'll forgive our sins and purge us of all wrongdoing. If we claim that we've never sinned, we out-and-out contradict God—make a liar out of him. A claim like that only shows off our ignorance of God" (The Message).

God will knock at your heart until you invite Him in. I love what Revelation 3:20–21 says: "Look at me. I stand at the door. I knock. If you hear me call and open the door, I'll come right in and sit down to supper with you. Conquerors will sit alongside me at the head table, just as I, having conquered, took the place of honor at the side of my Father. That's my gift to the conquerors!" (The Message). God will knock on the door of your life continually. Some people mistake that knock for condemnation. Yes, God will convict your heart of wrongdoing but not because He is angry with you. It's because He wants you to be free!

Second Peter 3:9 tells us that "the Lord is not slow in keeping his promise, as some understand slowness. He is patient with you, not wanting anyone to perish, but everyone to come to repentance." When you choose Christ, you are choosing freedom—freedom from loneliness, fear, insecurity, and so much more. But choosing to not serve God will cost you everything. Romans 6:22–23 says, "But now that you've found you don't have to listen to sin tell you what to do, and have discovered the delight of listening to God telling you, what a surprise! A whole, healed, put-together life right now, with more and more of life on the way! Work hard for sin your whole life and your pension is death. But God's gift is real life, eternal life, delivered by Jesus, our Master" (THE MESSAGE).

The New International Version puts verse 23 this way: "The wages of sin is death, but the gift of God is eternal life." In other words, your payday for sin should be death, but God gave us life through Christ Jesus! That means nothing can hold you back. Paul said it best in Philippians 3:10–11: "I gave up all that inferior stuff so I could know Christ personally, experience his resurrection power, be a partner in his suffering, and go all the way with him to death itself. If there was any way to get in on the resurrection from the dead, I wanted to do it" (THE MESSAGE).

GOD DOESN'T SEND ANYONE TO HELL

Today there is once again a huge controversy about the horrible and very real place called hell. I say once again because the controversy of whether hell is real has gone on for centuries. I would like to address that issue here. Many people would love to have you think hell is a state of mind, a state of being, or a place here on earth. This Universalist mentality challenges the very notion that a loving God would send people to hell to suffer damnation. Most of their arguments are half-truths that bring confusion, especially to those who want so badly to justify a lifestyle of sin or relieve themselves of the burden of thinking a soul could be doomed to spend eternity in hell.

Universalists declare, "Jesus conquered all sin on the cross, and thus we are all now accepted into heaven." This is partly true. He did conquer all sin on the cross, but that doesn't mean there is nothing left for you and me to do. It is a noble concept, but the idea that Jesus's death erased the possibility that anyone would experience hell is simply fantasy.

Universalists challenge whether the Bible teaches that people should fear eternal damnation or whether Satan has the power to win in some people's lives after what Jesus accomplished on the cross. They will say things such as, "Love wins," but that statement is factually incorrect. It is truth that actually wins. Love is an emotion that is very powerful, but truth conquers even our strongest emotions. Love will cause a man to abandon his family to pursue someone else's affections, but truth does not change with our emotional tides.

There are many references to hell in the Bible. Proverbs 12:28 says, "Good men and women travel right into life; sin's detours take you straight to hell" (THE MESSAGE). Sin will take you away from God's plan for your life every time. When Jesus died on the cross, He removed every excuse for us to choose the sin over Him. We must be determined not to give sin any place in our lives, as Mark 9:45 instructs us: "And if your foot causes you to stumble, cut it off. It is better for you to enter life crippled than to have two feet and be thrown into hell."

I want to declare to you this fact: *a loving God doesn't send anyone to hell!* A righteous and loving God made a way for you and me to avoid hell, but that plan shifted the responsibility to us. God has opened His arms wide for all of creation. He loves all of us with an everlasting love. He doesn't want anyone to perish. Yet with that being said, let me be very clear when I say that eternity in heaven is promised only to those who accept Christ.

God doesn't make us accept Him or force us to serve Him. He has given us the choice. That is what it means to have a free will. We are not robots or pawns in a cosmic chess game.

True love can be exercised only when two individuals choose to walk together. If I told my wife she had to love me, then I would never receive true love from her. True love works only when the agreement of love between the two individuals is matched with equal affection.

No matter how some may manipulate the Greek or Hebrew words for "hell," it is a very real place that was created for the devil and his minions. God did not create hell for you; the Bible is clear on this subject. God gave us a way to avoid hell—by proclaiming that Jesus Christ is our Lord and Savior (Rom. 10:9). God doesn't want any of us to go this horrible place of torment and pain, but the choice is ours to make.

Jesus is the only way to heaven, and we must accept that truth by faith in order to be saved. As theologian John Calvin said, "A man will be justified by faith when, excluded from the righteousness of works, he by faith lays hold of the righteousness of Christ, and clothed in it appears in the sight of God not as a sinner, but as righteous."[1]

Romans 5:6–8 paints a vivid picture of what Jesus did for us when He made it possible for us to spend eternity in heaven. "Christ arrives right on time to make this happen. He didn't, and doesn't, wait for us to get ready. He presented himself for this sacrificial death when we were far too weak and rebellious to do anything to get ourselves ready. And even if we hadn't been so weak, we wouldn't have known what to do anyway. We can understand someone dying for a person worth dying for, and we can understand how someone good and noble could inspire us to selfless sacrifice. But God put his love on the line for us by offering his Son in sacrificial death while we were of no use whatever to him" (THE MESSAGE). Does that sound like an angry God? It sounds to me like a God who loved us enough to put His life on the line!

We have been given this promise: "We follow this sequence in Scripture: The First Adam received life, the Last Adam is a life-giving Spirit. Physical life comes first, then spiritual—a firm base shaped from the earth, a final completion coming out of heaven. The First Man was made out of earth, and people since then are earthy; the Second Man was made out of heaven, and people now can be heavenly. In the same way that we've worked from our earthy origins, let's embrace our heavenly ends" (1 Cor. 15:45–49, The Message).

In Joshua 24:15 there is a powerful line that says, "Choose for yourselves this day whom you will serve." In other words, make a choice. I pray you will choose wisely. God wants you with Him!

Chapter 8

GOD DOESN'T THINK THE WAY WE DO

OD IS NOT what you imagined or what you think you understand. If you understand then you have failed."[1] I love that quote by St. Augustine. Since the beginning of time man has attempted to understand the mind of God. I imagine it has driven the wisest of men mad and the most arrogant of men to humility. We must understand that God doesn't think as we do. We are made in His image, but we will never truly grasp the intellect of an infinite God with our finite minds. Yet something amazing happens when we try to understand Him. When we try to comprehend the depth and reach of God, it forces us to go deeper in Him. We also will be forced to take Him out of the human box we so often try to keep God in.

We serve a huge God! He can span the universe with one hand. The prophet Isaiah said, "See, the Sovereign LORD comes with power, and his arm rules for him. See, his reward is with him, and his recompense accompanies him. He tends his flock like a shepherd: he gathers the lambs in his arms and carries them close to his heart; he gently leads those that have young" (Isa. 40:10–11). The passage in Isaiah shows both the powerful and loving sides of God, both the ruler and the pastor sides of His personality.

Isaiah goes even deeper into God's attributes when he

describes the size and intellect of God. He says, "Who has measured the waters in the hollow of his hand, or with the breadth of his hand marked off the heavens? Who has held the dust of the earth in a basket; or weighed the mountains on the scales and the hills in a balance? Who has understood the mind of the LORD, or instructed him as his counselor?" (Isa. 40:12–13). In other words, there is no one big enough to give God advice. He is not only the ruler of the heavens and earth—God is above all!

I shared these verses to reiterate that God doesn't think as you and I do. That is why it is so easy to have misconceptions about who He truly is as our Lord. First Corinthians 2:10–11 says, "God has revealed it to us by his Spirit. The Spirit searches all things, even the deep things of God. For who among men knows the thoughts of a man except the man's spirit within him? In the same way no one knows the thoughts of God except the Spirit of God."

Only God knows His own thoughts. Yet in the Christian world I hear people speak on God's behalf all the time. Many times they declare things about God that are opposite His Word. Yet the closest thing to God's résumé is His Word. Jesus was the Word made flesh, and that is why God never contradicts His Word. It is impossible for God to contradict Himself.

When we think things such as, "God doesn't like me" or "God is mad at me" or "God has forgotten me," we are believing concepts that are contrary to God's Word. But when we begin to understand the depths of God, we can see how we have misunderstood who He is to His creation. Look at what the apostle Paul said in Romans 11:33–36: "Have you ever come on anything quite like this extravagant generosity of God, this deep, deep wisdom? It's way over our heads. We'll never figure it out. Is there anyone around who can explain God? Anyone smart enough to tell him what to do? Anyone who has done him such a huge favor that God has to ask his advice? Everything comes from him; everything happens through him; everything ends up in him. Always glory! Always praise! Yes. Yes. Yes" (THE MESSAGE).

I love those verses. God truly is the author and finisher of our faith. The beginning and the end! The Alpha and Omega! I like the way poet Walt Whitman put it:

> I say to mankind, Be not curious about God.
> For I who am curious about each am not curious
>   about God
> (No array of terms can say how much I am at peace
>   about God and about death.)
> I hear and behold God in every object,
>   yet understand God not in the least.[2]

God doesn't think like us, but the good news is, He is moved by us! He understands everything we could go through! Hebrews 4:15 says, "For we do not have a high priest who is unable to sympathize with our weaknesses, but we have one who has been tempted in every way, just as we are—yet was without sin." The writer of Hebrews is giving us a glimpse into God's heart. He's letting us know that where we walk, God has walked. Yet He is still God. He remains holy and without sin.

So the next time you think you understand what God must be thinking, just stop, pray, read His Word, and listen for His voice. God still speaks. The more you listen for it, the more clearly you will hear it. And you will probably find that it sounds different than you thought it would. One of my favorite Bible passages of all time is Jeremiah 33:2–3: "This is GOD's Message, the God who made earth, made it livable and lasting, known everywhere as GOD: 'Call to me and I will answer you. I'll tell you marvelous and wondrous things that you could never figure out on your own'" (THE MESSAGE).

These are two of my favorite verses because I love to hear the voice of God. The voice of God can change everything!

RUN TO THE SECRET PLACE

There are times when I simply have no answers, when I am at a complete loss for what to do. But I have found that when I am in this place, I just need to get to that secret place with God. He created us in the secret place, and if we can find our way back to it, He will repair, restore, and instruct us there! God is calling us to get in a place where we will have our ears open to Him. There is no need to put on a religious production for God. Just get real with Him, and He will show you His plan for your life.

Look what Jesus said about getting away and spending time with God in prayer. "And when you come before God, don't turn that into a theatrical production either. All these people making a regular show out of their prayers, hoping for stardom! Do you think God sits in a box seat? Here's what I want you to do: Find a quiet, secluded place so you won't be tempted to role-play before God. Just be there as simply and honestly as you can manage. The focus will shift from you to God, and you will begin to sense his grace" (Matt. 6:5–6, The Message).

God will literally change your focus! That means He will change your thought patterns. Something powerful takes place when I go into prayer. I can go in worried about my issue but come out understanding that God has a perfect plan! God doesn't think like us, but He loves it when we press in to find out what He is thinking. He isn't an unresponsive God but rather a God who is looking to respond!

No matter what you're walking through, He is right there with you. In fact, God has a prayer life Himself, and it includes you. As we saw earlier, Psalm 42:7–8 tells us our lives are God's prayer. Regardless of the hour God is there. He is your Friend, and as you'll soon see, He wants you to be His friend too.

Chapter 9

GOD WANTS TO BE OUR FRIEND

G OD IS LOOKING for a friend. He needs us as much as we need Him, and He would never reject the very ones with whom He desires friendship.

The Bible tells us that God had close friends. The Book of James says "'Abraham believed God, and it was credited to him as righteousness,' and he was called God's friend" (James 2:23). In Exodus we read that the Lord would show up in Moses's tent and "speak to Moses face to face, as a man speaks with his friend" (Exod. 33:11).

Passages such as these show that God is more than our deity. He is a personal and close friend. We see throughout Scripture that God put people in relationship: Paul and Timothy; Ruth and Naomi; Elijah and Elisha; Peter, James, and John; David and Jonathan. These relationships were no accident; God does not want us to do life alone. What's more, these human relationships are just a snapshot of the kind of relationship He wants to have with us. God longs to be in relationship with us, yet His heart is so often misunderstood, and many people do not realize that. In fact, they often think the exact opposite.

When I was growing up I was never told that I could be God's friend. I thought, "Surely God is too busy to be my friend!" The Bible says that we are created in His image (Gen.

1:27). We know that God is not flesh and blood but Spirit. And we know that He is three in one—Father, Son, and Holy Spirit. Just as He is in relationship with the Trinity—they are distinct persons but in constant fellowship and complete unity—so does He want to be in relationship with us, the finishing touch on His creation. This is why He created us—so He could have a relationship with us. He enjoys it when we spend time with Him, and He longs for our worship. In fact, in Genesis 1:31 He was so pleased when He made mankind that He said that "it was very good."

Angels are on assignment. They take orders from God then carry out His commands. God wants us to walk in obedience toward Him too, a topic we will address in a later chapter, but He placed in us an ability to choose right and wrong. He gave us the ability to think, dream, and praise—and He did that on purpose. God created the angels to do His bidding, but He created us to commune with Him.

The Bible says in Genesis 3:8 that God and Adam walked together in the cool of the evening. I often speak at men's conferences, and I've found that there is nothing more powerful than when a man begins to understand that God wants to be his friend. Most men are always at war—with themselves or something else. They spend their days searching for purpose. Most simply do not know how to relax. What they must realize is that they will never find their purpose until they understand that God has a plan for them—and that plan includes friendship with Him.

I often tell people that men drive to work fast and drive home slowly. The reason they drive home slowly is that they need time to walk through their day and reflect on what happened. When I speak to groups of men, I tell them that God still wants to walk with them in the cool of the evening, just as He walked with Adam. He will get in the car with them and be their friend. All they need to do is acknowledge that He is there. When they invite God into their cars, He will hang out and minister to them. He will listen and give good advice, because He is a friend.

GOD IS NOT A FAIR-WEATHER FRIEND

Has anyone ever told you he didn't want to be your friend anymore? Those words can cut to the heart. Being hurt by a friend can impact your current and future relationships. In order to fully realize that God isn't mad at us, one must understand the kind of friend God is to us. Romans 11:28–29 says, "From your point of view as you hear and embrace the good news of the Message, it looks like the Jews are God's enemies. But looked at from the long-range perspective of God's overall purpose, they remain God's oldest friends. God's gifts and God's call are under full warranty—never canceled, never rescinded" (THE MESSAGE).

God doesn't change His mind about us. He is a true friend. The promise made in Romans 11 is not only for the Jews of Bible days. Jesus has made it possible for us to also walk in covenant with God. That means the promise extends to us too when we accept Christ's gift of salvation!

Years ago my family went through a rough season in ministry. I had moved the family and ministry to Las Vegas, Nevada, in hope of enlarging our organization. Soon after our move my wife and I realized that it was not God's plan for our life. I had missed it big-time. I have learned that *the calling of God, without the timing of God, results in the absence of God!* Ambition and passion got in the way of wisdom and proper planning.

Despite that, our family grew closer in every aspect of our relationships during that season. More importantly I grew closer to God. I became more reliant on God than I had ever been in my life. It was truly the best of times and the worst of times. It was during this season that God gave me a revelation that He wants to be our friend, not just our Savior and Lord.

I was driving home from the airport one day when a song came on the radio. The singer was one of my favorite musicians, Israel Houghton, and the song began with Israel simply asking God who we humans are that He would be mindful of us and hear us when we call out to Him. Then later in the song Israel declared over and over that we are friends of God—that He calls us His friends. Those lyrics were unbelievable to me. God called me His friend?

I had to pull over to the side of the road because this song was ministering to me so deeply. God began to speak to me and give me direction for both my family and the ministry. It was one of those powerful moments of revelation straight from heaven. That was the day I realized God truly is my friend. I realized that He cared about me, that He loved me, and that He wanted to spend time with me and give me the direction I so desperately needed.

I must have played that song a thousand times over the next few months. My heart's cry is to always be a friend of God. That's one reason I love Proverbs 22:11: "He who loves a pure heart and whose speech is gracious will have the king for his friend." If there's one thing I know for sure it's that I want the King to be my friend.

We were created for God's pleasure. You and I were not created to be robots. We were not created to be a statistic, to live a life filled with pain, or to feel like nobodies in life. We were created to enjoy the love of God and praise Him. Revelation 4:11 proclaims that our God is worthy to receive glory and honor and power, because He created all things and by His will all things were created and have their being.

God desires to walk with us and help us. Psalm 16:11 says God makes known to us the path of life, and He will fill us with joy in His presence, with eternal pleasures at His right hand. How could we not praise a God like that!

Friends Spend Time Together

The key to true friendship is quality time. God loves to spend time with us, and He loves to spend that time in the secret place. The Bible says in Psalm 139:13 that He created us in the secret place, which is His presence, and He wants us to go back to the secret place to spend time with Him. In the secret place we will find everything we need. Psalm 91:1–2 says, "He who dwells in the secret place of the Most High shall abide under the shadow of the Almighty. I will say of the Lord, 'He is my refuge and my fortress; my God, in Him I will trust'" (nkjv).

When we are in the secret place, God wants our focus to be on Him. He wants our undivided attention. God doesn't like to share. Exodus 34:14 exhorts us not to worship any other god, "for the Lord, whose name is Jealous, is a jealous God."

When we spend time in God's presence, He will speak to us and share His secrets. Jeremiah 33:2–3 says, "This is God's Message, the God who made earth, made it livable and lasting, known everywhere as God: 'Call to me and I will answer you. I'll tell you marvelous and wondrous things that you could never figure out on your own.'" How cool is that? I have found this to be true so many times in my life. When I cannot figure something out, if I go to the secret place, God will reveal the answer to me.

He knows just what I need. He is a personal God. As Psalm 6:9 says, the Lord hears our cry for mercy and He accepts our prayers. All we have to do is seek Him. When we do, we will find Him! Jeremiah 29:13 affirms this when it says, "You will seek me and find me when you seek me with all your heart."

God has given us an open invitation to come to Him. He wants us to be like the psalmist who wrote, "And here I am, your invited guest—it's incredible! I enter your house; here I am, prostrate in your inner sanctum, waiting for directions to get me safely through enemy lines" (Ps. 5:7–8, The Message).

Because God is a real friend, we can trust that He always has our best interests in mind as He directs our path.

Like any relationship, friendship takes work on both sides. My mom used to say, "You have to be a friend if you want to have a friend!" There is so much truth in that statement. I've told students for years, "Show me your friends, and I will show you your future!" God wants you in His house with Him. He wants you close to Him, and He will protect you.

He cares when you are in pain. He will rescue you and has provided healing for your body, spirit, and soul! Psalm 34:18 promises, "If your heart is broken, you'll find God right there; if you're kicked in the gut, he'll help you catch your breath" (THE MESSAGE). A true friend is always there to help! That is who our God is to His creation!

God is the friend who will be there when you have no one else! This truth hit home for my family a few months ago when my little girl, Abby, went to my wife, Karen, and shared something amazing. She said, "Mommy, last night I had another dream." Karen said, "What do you mean, Abby? What type of dream did you have?" She said, "Jesus came to see me in my dream. He used to do that when I was in the orphanage sleeping with the other children in my crib." This, of course, melted Karen's heart. In the years since we'd brought Abby home from China, she had never shared this before.

Karen asked Abby what Jesus had said to her in the dream. She said, "Well, Jesus used to come and see me in the orphanage in my dreams and tell me to hold on because my mommy would soon be here to get me." At this point Karen was in tears. Abby went on to say, "And last night He came and saw me again. He said, 'See, Abby, I told you your mommy would come and get you!'"

Karen was in shock as Abby said, "Isn't that neat, Mommy?" Of course, Karen, with tears streaming down her face, wrapped our little angel in her arms. That was more than "neat." It was a beautiful image of the real heart of God—and out of the mouth of a babe! God takes care of us all. That is what I call a friend!

THE MARKS OF TRUE FRIENDSHIP

It is so hard to explain friendship with God to someone who has a hard time maintaining friendships. No one modeled friendship better than Jesus. By getting a healthy understanding of friendship as Jesus taught it, we will deepen our grasp of our friendship with God.

First, true friendship is covenantal, not contractual. In other words, because of the covenant God made with us His children, He will always be there for us, even if we were to reject Him. The relationship is not conditional. There is no "If you do this, then I will do that" mind-set with God. I don't know about you, but that's a relief to me!

Second, true friendship is sacrificial. Think about this: Jesus chose to die for you when you didn't even know Him. Look what Jesus said about true friendship in John 15:12–13: "My command is this: Love each other as I have loved you. Greater love has no one than this, that he lay down his life for his friends." Jesus declared that a true friend understands love and is always willing to lay his life down for his friend.

Third, true friendship is reciprocated. Jesus went on to say in John 15, "You are my friends if you do what I command. I no longer call you servants, because a servant does not know his master's business. Instead, I have called you friends, for everything that I learned from my Father I have made known to you" (vv. 14–15). Jesus was letting the disciples know that they had a deep relationship with Him, and He expected them to reciprocate that relationship with others. This is how people would come to discover the true heart of God.

The reason Jesus taught about the importance of friendship is because it enables us to have victory in the Spirit realm. In

Matthew 18:18–20 Jesus said, "I tell you the truth, whatever you bind on earth will be bound in heaven, and whatever you loose on earth will be loosed in heaven. Again, I tell you that if two of you on earth agree about anything you ask for, it will be done for you by my Father in heaven. For where two or three come together in my name, there am I with them."

Jesus is saying that when we walk in covenant together He will join in with us. That should be good news to us—news worth shouting about—but the fact of the matter is, most people have no idea what friendship means. They have never been taught the rules and regulations governing friendships, so they are not prepared to walk in the kind of agreement that brings breakthrough in the spirit. So below I have listed twenty important precepts that will help define what true friendship is.

1. A true friend always desires to see the other friends prosper.

2. A friend doesn't join another friend's folly (Prov. 5:23).

3. A true friend always watches out for the good of his friend.

4. A friend is never chosen by personality alone but according to God's purpose (Rom. 8:28).

5. A friend never gets in the way of another friend's relationship with Christ (Heb. 10:24).

6. A friend understands boundaries and convictions.

7. A friend always allows his friends to make mistakes (Prov. 17:17).

8. A true friend always looks for a way to restore a fallen friend (Eccles. 4:10).

9. A friend understands how to keep a confidence.

10. A friend understands the importance of widening the circle.

11. A friend can be trusted.

12. A friend has no agenda.

13. A friend has good dreams for his friend.

14. A friend always loves enough to be honest.

15. A friend stays clear of the "off-limit" areas.

16. A friend knows how to perform CPR on another friend when he has died spiritually (Job 16:20–21).

17. A friend never feeds the other friend's weaknesses.

18. A friend understands that love covers a multitude of sins.

19. A friend is in it for the long haul.

20. A friend pushes the other friend to go deeper spiritually (Prov. 27:17).

God loves it when we choose right relationships. Here is a great life equation: right relationships will produce right choices, which create right moments in God's presence.

Did you know that when you spend time with a fellow believer, God takes notice? In fact, when two believers talk about spiritual things together, God joins in! Malachi 3:16 says, "Then those who feared the LORD talked with each other, and the LORD listened and heard." God made us for relationship—with Him and with others.

Chapter 10

GOD AND JESUS ARE ONE

W HO'S YOUR DADDY?" That is something I often say
to my son when we're playing video games, football, Ping-Pong, or any other game and I score. I
like to have fun with Nate, but one day he turned the tables
on me when I made that statement after scoring during one
of our marathon basketball games. Instead of just laughing
off the jab, Nate replied, "Well, Dad, you are!" It was funny
then, but Nate's response also touched on a truth that I pray
anyone who thinks God is mad at him will open up his heart
to receive.

You see, though my son and I are different people, we are
very much alike. We both are serious competitors, we both
love seeing lives changed, we both love to help the hurting,
and we both live our lives passionately, as if we are racing
against time. Yet we each have different gifts and unique
qualities. For instance, my son is a much better athlete than I
am and a whole lot smarter than me, but I have gifts he does
not have. My son came from me, yet his lot in life is different
from mine.

I think sometimes as Christians we notice the ways God
and Jesus are different but forget the fact that they are actually one. I believe many people see Jesus as a loving shepherd

with a lamb on His shoulder, or they see Him with scars on His hands or as a baby in a manger.

Then there is God, whom they see as an old, Father Time-looking figure who moves us like pawns on the chessboard of life. They see Him as a mixture of a mythical Greek god and Santa Claus—a huge, imposing figure with a flowing beard. Jesus is the loving, kind intercessor, and God is more of a mighty force of nature who speaks through thunder and lightning. This is why it is easy for people to think Jesus loves them and God is mad at them.

We have come to separate Jesus from God, but they are one and the same. The Trinity is made up of three—Father, Son, and Holy Spirit—and the three are all one. I know this can seem confusing, so let's look at the way Jesus explained His relationship with the Father during a conversation with His disciple Phillip.

> Jesus said, "I am the Road, also the Truth, also the Life. No one gets to the Father apart from me. If you really knew me, you would know my Father as well. From now on, you do know him. You've even seen him!" Philip said, "Master, show us the Father; then we'll be content." "You've been with me all this time, Philip, and you still don't understand? To see me is to see the Father. So how can you ask, 'Where is the Father?' Don't you believe that I am in the Father and the Father is in me? The words that I speak to you aren't mere words. I don't just make them up on my own. The Father who resides in me crafts each word into a divine act."
>
> —John 14:6–10, The Message

Jesus was saying, "Hey, the Father and I are the same." This is critical to our understanding of who our Father truly is to His children.

God sent Himself to die on the cross. Mankind was

separated from God because of sin, and each year a priest had
to make a sacrifice to atone for the sins of the people. Because
of sin, we couldn't get to God and have a personal relationship with Him, so the Father sent Jesus to stand in His place
and pay the penalty for our sins. Jesus died as our ransom.
Then He created a new covenant so we could have access to
the Father. Hebrews 9:15 tells us, "For this reason Christ is
the mediator of a new covenant, that those who are called
may receive the promised eternal inheritance—now that he
has died as a ransom to set them free from the sins committed
under the first covenant."

Though Jesus was fully God while He walked the earth,
He cried out to His Father every day. We see one of these
moments of prayer in Luke 10:21, when Jesus rejoiced with
the Father. Jesus never lost sight of who His Father was, and
He placed Himself under the Father's complete authority. By
submitting to the Father's direction and oversight, Jesus willingly sacrificed His life on the cross, thus giving us access to
the Father.

Jesus went on to say in John 14, "Believe me when I say that
I am in the Father and the Father is in me; or at least believe
on the evidence of the miracles themselves. I tell you the
truth, anyone who has faith in me will do what I have been
doing. He will do even greater things than these, because I
am going to the Father. And I will do whatever you ask in my
name, so that the Son may bring glory to the Father. You may
ask me for anything in my name, and I will do it" (vv. 11–14).
Jesus was saying that if you ask Him, then you are asking the
Father and vice versa. They are the same.

If you view God as some ogre waiting for you to mess up,
then you will always think He is mad at you. But when you
realize He loved you enough to send His Son to die for your
sins, then you will realize what a loving and awesome Dad
you have.

While Jesus was hanging on the cross, suspended between

heaven and earth, He cried out to His Father in a loud voice, "*Eloi, Eloi, lama sabachthani?*'—which means, 'My God, my God, why have you forsaken me?'" (Matt. 27:46). We know that the Father sent the Son to suffer on the cross, so why would God, if He is a good Dad, abandon His Son?

In that verse Jesus was experiencing the punishment that you and I deserved. He bore all of our sin and took the judgment that was meant for you and me. Second Corinthians 5:21 says, "God made him who had no sin to be sin for us, so that in him we might become the righteousness of God." Jesus took our place, thus opening the door for us to be in communion with God the Father. In other words, God's only begotten Son bore the sin that made God mad so we could experience the amazing love He has for the sons and daughters He created.

God isn't mad at us—He loves us! We now have access to Him as the righteous sons and daughters of God. We belong to Him. He is our Dad. Galatians 4:6 says, "You can tell for sure that you are now fully adopted as his own children because God sent the Spirit of his Son into our lives crying out, 'Papa! Father!'" (THE MESSAGE). So the next time someone says to you, "Who's your Daddy?" you can say, "God, the Father in heaven, who resides in my heart!"

Chapter 11

GOD DISCIPLINES THOSE HE LOVES

A TRUE FATHER UNDERSTANDS discipline. Yet disciplining a child is one of the hardest things a parent has to do. Once before he punished me, I remember my father saying, "This is going to hurt me more than it hurts you!" He meant it, but, of course, at the time I really did not agree. I wanted to shout, "Then don't do it! Step away from that belt!"

I understood what he meant years later when I became a father. My son, Nate, was always a great kid, but from time to time he would be mischievous or allow his tongue to get him in trouble. On one particular occasion he had gotten into trouble several days in a row for talking in class. What can I say? He definitely came by this honestly. All of my report cards said, "Talks too much and daydreams too much!" I always say my report cards just prophesied my future!

Nate's teacher sent home a note saying she was having trouble with his constant talking. When my wife received the note from Nate's teacher, she informed me that after so many warnings, it was time for a spanking. So Nate and I went into his bedroom for his day of reckoning.

Just before I started to spank him, I looked into my son's big green eyes and instantly saw my reflection. I told Nate to look into my eyes, and I asked him, "What do you see?"

Nate responded, "I see me!" I told him, "That is exactly right." I told him that I was in him and he was in me, and that I understood that some of the issues in my life would probably show up in his. I told him that as his father, I had to help him get free of anything that could hold him back from reaching his potential.

We wept and prayed together. It was a turning point in our relationship. I ended up not spanking him that day because I knew he had learned his lesson. It was the last time he got in trouble at school.

A true father disciplines with love and purpose. It is easy to think God is angry with you if you don't understand the role of discipline. God is not anti-fun, but He doesn't want us to make choices that will cause us pain. Proverbs 15:10 says, "Stern discipline awaits him who leaves the path; he who hates correction will die." In other words, discipline actually saves a person's life. But it is equally important to remember that discipline without relationship breeds rebellion.

One of the great misconceptions in today's society is that a loving father gives his children the freedom to do whatever they want and that he will cover the consequences for them. The fact is that disciplining a child who messes up is often as important as giving him a hug when he scores a soccer goal. Proper restorative discipline comes from the heart of a parent who wants to lovingly guide his child to become a good and godly human being.

That means as a parent I have to always be aware of the power I possess to shape my children's lives. I am always careful to speak in love and not anger. Proverbs 15:1 says, "A gentle response defuses anger, but a sharp tongue kindles a temper-fire" (THE MESSAGE).

I must also be willing to establish boundaries because they will help my children grow. What do I mean? Boundaries create a place to stop and begin. In their great book *Boundaries* Dr. Henry Cloud and Dr. John Townsend talk about the important role consequences play in bringing needed changes in our lives. They write that correct discipline = freedom = choices = consequences = love.[1] Not allowing a person to experience the consequences of his actions can interrupt the character-building process. Many times this process is painful, but bad character doesn't change until the consequences land. It is better to prepare your kids than to have to repair your kids!

It's natural for us to want to prove that we can make it on our own. God gives us the freedom to do just that, but I have learned the more freedom we possess, the more guidance we actually need. Freedom without discipline is dangerous. The Father allows us to make our own choices, but He wants us to let Him take over our lives. The apostle Paul said it well in his letter to the church in Rome.

> Those who think they can do it on their own end up obsessed with measuring their own moral muscle but never get around to exercising it in real life. Those who trust God's action in them find that God's Spirit is in them—living and breathing God! Obsession with self in these matters is a dead end; attention to God leads us out into the open, into a spacious, free life. Focusing on the self is the opposite of focusing on God. Anyone completely absorbed in self ignores God, ends up thinking more about self than God. That person ignores who God is and what he is doing. And God isn't pleased at being ignored. But if God himself has taken up residence in your life, you can hardly be thinking more of yourself than of him. Anyone, of course, who has not welcomed this invisible but clearly present God, the Spirit of Christ, won't know what we're talking about. But for you who welcome him, in whom he dwells—even though you still experience all the limitations of sin—you yourself experience life on God's terms. It stands to reason, doesn't

it, that if the alive-and-present God who raised Jesus from the dead moves into your life, he'll do the same thing in you that he did in Jesus, bringing you alive to himself? When God lives and breathes in you (and he does, as surely as he did in Jesus), you are delivered from that dead life. With his Spirit living in you, your body will be as alive as Christ's!

—ROMANS 8:5–11, THE MESSAGE

When God the Father takes over, your life isn't about what you want anymore. It becomes about what God has planned for you. That sometimes creates a need for God to discipline us. The passage in Romans 8 said He doesn't like to be ignored! In other words, God demands our attention and respect. That doesn't mean He doesn't love us or that He is mad at us; rather, it means He cares for us. God loves us enough to allow us the freedom to make decisions. But the choices we make bring consequence. Freedom isn't exactly free.

If you're paying the price for your choices because God is trying to teach you something, that is proof of His love for you. Hebrews 12:7–11 says, "Endure hardship as discipline; God is treating you as sons. For what son is not disciplined by his father? If you are not disciplined (and everyone undergoes discipline), then you are illegitimate children and not true sons. Moreover, we have all had human fathers who disciplined us and we respected them for it. How much more should we submit to the Father of our spirits and live! Our fathers disciplined us for a little while as they thought best; but God disciplines us for our good, that we may share in his holiness. No discipline seems pleasant at the time, but painful. Later on, however, it produces a harvest of righteousness and peace for those who have been trained by it."

God allows us to walk through things so we can grow and find true freedom from anything keeping us from God's plan for our lives. The Father has created boundaries and guidelines for us to live by. If we choose to do our own thing, there will be consequences. The Bible says in 1 Samuel 15:22 that "obedience is better than sacrifice" (NLT). God expects us to obey His Word and apply it to our lives. When I get to heaven, my goal is to arrive with nothing left to accomplish. That means I need to be obedient to what God instructs me to do, because I have learned that I will only go as far as the level of my obedience.

The apostle Paul continually tried to convince the Corinthian church that God had more for them. He knew he was fighting against a cultural war, so he reminded the Corinthians that God had a better plan: "Do you see the difference? Sacrifices offered to idols are offered to nothing, for what's the idol but a nothing? Or worse than nothing, a minus, a demon! I don't want you to become part of something that reduces you to less than yourself. And you can't have it both ways, banqueting with the Master one day and slumming with demons the next. Besides, the Master won't put up with it. He wants us—all or nothing. Do you think you can get off with anything less?" (1 Cor. 10:19–22, The Message).

God wants all or nothing. He doesn't want to share you. So when we experience God's discipline, it is really His protection. Discipline doesn't equal anger; it is evidence of the Father's love. God wants to see us restored when we've fallen away from His plan for us (Gal. 6:1–2), but He also has called us to take responsibility for our actions. That is why He expects us to do all we can to live in accordance with God's Word. He gives us these boundaries to protect us from pain. Galatians 6:4–5 tells us, "Each one should test his own actions. Then he can take pride in himself, without comparing himself to somebody else, for each one should carry his own load." God expects us to carry our own load! He expects us to be responsible and make right choices.

God gave us a map for life. It's called the Bible. We have to follow it. Hebrews 4:12 tells us, "The word of God is living and active. Sharper than any double-edged sword, it pene-trates even to dividing soul and spirit, joints and marrow; it judges the thoughts and attitudes of the heart."

We can't pick and choose what to believe. In fact, the Bible says for us to not take away or add to God's Word. Revelation 22:19 issues a stern warning against picking and choosing what we like from Scripture. "And if anyone takes words away from this book of prophecy, God will take away from him his share in the tree of life and in the holy city, which are described in this book."

When we read God's Word, it begins to perform surgery in our lives. It cuts out, adds to, and heals! The apostle Paul declared in Romans 11:22 that we must "consider therefore the kindness and sternness of God: sternness to those who fell, but kindness to you, provided that you continue in his kindness. Otherwise, you also will be cut off." Experiencing the stern love of God is not a sign that the Father is angry with you. It is the opposite. It is proof that He loves you too much to let you continue down a path that could harm you.

Chapter 12

GOD WANTS US TO BE BLESSED

I F GOD LOVES me, then why did I lose my dream home? He must be mad at me!" I actually heard those words from a dear friend. We are living in difficult times in our nation. Economic hardship has impacted not only the rough neighborhoods but also the affluent. Foreclosure signs litter yards from California to Florida. The housing crisis has been no respecter of persons.

To make matters worse, at the time of this writing US unemployment hovered above 8 percent,[1] and the percentage of Americans on food stamps had grown to roughly 15 percent (or around 45 million people).[2] In today's economy no news is almost good news. Where is God the Father in all of this? Has He abandoned our nation? Has He somehow turned a blind eye to people's pain? Are we still one nation under God?

Recently I wrote a blog called "Is Jesus America's Mascot?"[3] I wrote that blog because it seemed to me that during the tough times we are facing in our nation, the people of God should react differently than we have been. If this really is a Christian nation, then during times of persecution or lack we should be on our faces crying out to the One who truly hears our cries.

"In God We Trust" became our nation's motto in 1956 and

was reaffirmed by Congress on November 1, 2011. Although many, including our president, thought the vote was just political posturing by a Republican-led House of Representatives,[4] I believe it was a great reminder of the fact that our nation is indeed a Christian nation. Yet I still have to ask, Do we really trust God? Before I go further into God's concern for your finances, I want to share a segment of the blog I wrote.

> During the turmoil we are now living in, if God is who we trust, I believe with all my heart the churches of America would be filled to the brim with a nation crying out for God. God must be so much more. He must be our Lord! Psalm 33:12 says, "Blessed is the nation whose God is the LORD, the people He chose for His inheritance." Throughout history, when things get rough, a nation can turn in one of two directions. The nation can head down the devastating road of secularism, where elitist people declare that man can fix our issues, or we can turn to God as our answer.
>
> I believe we are so close to an awakening. I see desperation for Jesus in services. I see a generation that has had enough of no Salt and Light religion. There is a cry coming from the mountains, plains, and shores for an encounter with Jesus. We the church must rise up. It is time for a crying out from the pulpit to the pews, from the subway to the dirt roads, from the schools to the courts that Jesus is our Lord. Now is when we truly decide if we are a nation that trusts in God, or if we trust in the corners of Wall and Broad Street.
>
> God loves America, but He loves all nations on the earth. What separates our nation is that we put God up in plain sight. We call on Him for our answers. If we are to be the city on the hill and the beacon of hope, we must open the door for Him to come in. Revelation 3:20 declares that He is knocking at our doors. Will we answer? The wickedness of this world

is increasing. The clock is ticking on liberty and justice for all! Israel is waiting for us to rise up while Islam knocks at their doors. From Beijing to Moscow they are watching to see if we truly believe what we have declared for over 200 years.

The question is this, is God just a mascot that we parade out to motivate an electorate, or is He our King? There are millions in our great nation who are ready to see God pour out His Spirit. From pulpits to Bible studies to students at flagpoles, there is a cry for heaven to invade earth. I still believe that "in God we trust," but we must not just parade Him out to motivate the electorates and try to win another moral victory. He must become our very breath!

God spoke these five things to my heart:

1. We must get our joy back. Psalm 45:7 says, "You love righteousness and hate wickedness; therefore God, your God, has set you above your companions by anointing you with the oil of joy." The joy of the Lord truly is our strength. No joy means no strength!

2. We must exercise our God-given authority. Colossians 2:10 says, "And you have been given fullness in Christ, who is the head over every power and authority."

3. We must realize that we are overcomers. Luke 10:19 says, "I have given you authority to trample on snakes and scorpions and to overcome all the power of the enemy; nothing will harm you." An overcomer always makes sure to insert his influence in all situations.

4. We must pray and cry out to God. Second Chronicles 7:14 gives this promise with a condition, "If my people, who are called by my name, will humble themselves and pray and seek my face and turn from their wicked ways, then will I hear from heaven and will forgive their sin and will heal their land." We must seek Him, and we will find Him.

5. Give Him access to move in our daily routines of life. Acts 17:28 says, "For in him we live and move and have our being." He wants to interrupt us. That doesn't mean we have to lose excellence in place of anointing. I love what a dear pastor and mentor named George Sawyer told me about his church: "We believe in anointed excellence." We must give Him access to the inner sanctums of our offices, living rooms, bedrooms, cars, and sanctuaries.

God is calling all of His pastors, influencers, and churches, with the hand of God upon them, to call for a Holy Spirit revolution! Together we can take our nation back! It first must start on our knees! For too long the media, the pundits, and philosophers have set the spiritual climate. We must declare Jesus from the rooftops. This is the moment the church has been awaiting!

We must be the Statue of Liberty to the world! Our mantra must be, "Give me your tired (Matt. 11:28), your poor (James 1:27), your huddled masses (Acts 1:8) yearning to breathe free (Acts 2:4)." Let the breath of God breathe life into the lungs of all believers! He breathed into the lungs of man in the garden and will do so again in their garages! It's great to have God on our T-shirts and money but even greater to have Him on our thrones!

Remember to keep your eyes on Jesus! Matthew 24:12–14 gives a warning and a promise that "because of the increase of wickedness, the love of most will grow cold, but he who stands firm to the end will be saved. And this gospel of the kingdom will be preached in the whole world as a testimony to all nations, and then the end will come."[5]

I shared that blog for a reason. Yes, our nation needs an awakening, and yes, God is calling to us to walk in His freedom, but I also believe the Father takes great care of His children. If you're going through a difficult economic situation, it is an opportunity to experience for you God's love and profound protection. He has your back. I realize that losing a job or home can be devastating to a person's lifestyle and psyche, but that isn't the time to turn away from God. It is the time to lean on Him. Let Him walk with you. This didn't happen because He is mad at you, though I believe God will use our circumstances to correct or guide our motives.

The simple truth is God promises to bless you. This is the promise found in Proverbs 3:5–12: "Trust God from the bottom of your heart; don't try to figure out everything on your own. Listen for God's voice in everything you do, everywhere you go; he's the one who will keep you on track. Don't assume that you know it all. Run to God! Run from evil! Your body will glow with health, your very bones will vibrate with life! Honor God with everything you own; give him the first and the best. Your barns will burst, your wine vats will brim over. But don't, dear friend, resent God's discipline; don't sulk under his loving correction. It's the child he loves that GOD corrects; a father's delight is behind all this" (THE MESSAGE).

Did you notice that the passage says the Father's delight is behind all this? Even God's correction is always from the heart of a Father who cares. You see, there have been times when I have had to discipline my children, but I promise it was always done in love. Many times when God is correcting our path it hurts, but He does it to protect us. The New International Version translates Proverbs 3:5–6 this way: "Trust in the LORD with all your heart and lean not on your own understanding; in all your ways acknowledge him, and he shall direct your paths straight."

The Bible tells us that our understanding will limit us. Instead, during the good and bad times we have to always trust God, always acknowledge Him, and always walk in obedience.

Pastor George Sawyer of Calvary Assembly of God in

Decatur, Alabama, whom I mentioned in my blog, recently made a powerful statement. He said, "Suddenlies are always preceded by obedience!"[6] I love that. If I simply do what God asks me to do, He will take care of the rest. He knows what I need. One way He responds to my obedience is by giving me a clear path to walk.

So many times our financial situations make us doubt God's goodness and think He has forgotten us. What we have to realize is that God enjoys seeing His children blessed. He doesn't want us to be broke! In fact, I have learned that He gets joy out of seeing us prosper. Psalm 35:27 says, "Let those who favor my righteous cause and have pleasure in my uprightness shout for joy and be glad and say continually, Let the Lord be magnified, Who takes pleasure in the prosperity of His servant" (AMP).

God doesn't want me or my children to suffer, and the same is true of you. Jesus even declared in John 6:35, "I am the bread of life. He who comes to me will never go hungry, and he who believes in me will never be thirsty." God will supply all of our needs, but I believe that many times our finances suffer because we are not using wisdom or not flowing with God's plan, which is best for us, and therefore we bear the consequences.

YOU ARE NOT FORGOTTEN

God has His eyes on you. He is watching you. He knows how to handle your most trying situation. Luke 12:6–7 says, "What's the price of two or three pet canaries? Some loose change, right? But God never overlooks a single one. And he pays even greater attention to you, down to the last detail— even numbering the hairs on your head! So don't be intimidated by all this bully talk. You're worth more than a million canaries" (THE MESSAGE).

The first few years Karen and I were married, it seemed

we always struggled financially. It was mostly because we had never learned wisdom and self-control in how we managed money. No one had mentored us in this area, and it showed. There were times when we avoided the phone calls from creditors and watched as the bills stacked up on the counter. We would walk heavyhearted and even in anger because of our financial situation. Eventually this attitude spilled over into our view of life and ministry. After a while it even affected our dreams.

Then one day we said to each other, "Enough is enough." The number one cause of divorce in America is finances. Money can control everything about you. It definitely can prevent a person from having the right view of God. Karen and I began to budget, plan, pray, give, and use wisdom in our spending. After twenty-two years of marriage we have learned that no matter what we face, there are three absolutes we will live by in our finances.

1. We will give.

My wife and I believe tithing is a New Testament command. The law of the Old Testament covenant is broken into three sections: civil law, ceremonial law, and moral law. Although we are no longer under the civil and ceremonial law of the old covenant, Jesus said we should keep the moral law, and tithing is part of that moral law. The New Testament does not teach tithing because it assumes people tithe. *It is a given.* Abraham and Jacob tithed long before Moses ever received the law (Gen. 28:22; Heb. 7:8–9), and we are still called to bring God our tithe. Tithing is not a legalistic act; it reflects a thankful heart that wants to give back to God what He has given to us.

But tithing is just the beginning. One of my favorite quotes is from the great evangelist Billy Graham in his sermon "Partners With God": "One of the greatest sins in America today is the fact that we are robbing God of that which rightfully belongs to Him. When we don't tithe, we shirk a just debt. Actually we are not giving when we give God one-tenth, for it belongs to Him already (Lev. 27:30). This is a debt we owe. Not until we have given a tenth do we actually begin making an offering to the Lord!"[7]

God doesn't need our money. He has cattle on a thousand hills (Ps. 50:10), and Psalm 24 says the whole earth belongs to Him. Giving is for our benefit. We are to give financially because our treasure does not belong stored up here on earth. Jesus said in Matthew 6:19–21, "Do not store up for yourselves treasures on earth, where moth and rust destroy, and where thieves break in and steal. But store up for yourselves treasures in heaven, where moth and rust do not destroy, and where thieves do not break in and steal. For where your treasure is, there your heart will be also."

The Bible also tells us that our giving pushes the devil back. I have found that when I am faithful in giving financially, God protects me. God says in Malachi 3:8–11, "Begin by being honest. Do honest people rob God? But you rob me day after day. You ask, 'How have we robbed you?' The tithe and the offering—that's how! And now you're under a curse—the whole lot of you—because you're robbing me. Bring your full tithe to the Temple treasury so there will be ample provisions in my Temple. Test me in this and see if I don't open up heaven itself to you and pour out blessings beyond your wildest dreams. For my part, I will defend you against marauders, protect your wheat fields and vegetable gardens against plunderers" (THE MESSAGE).

I am reminded of a time when I was taking an early morning flight. Karen called a few minutes before takeoff, frantic because someone was trying to break into our home. The plane was in taxi mode. All I could do was call some staff to get to my house immediately. For thirty minutes I was in the air, and all I could do was pray. I remember praying,

"Father, we are tithers. Today I am asking You to rebuke the devourer at my front door! Protect my family!"

When I finally landed, I called home immediately and found out everything was fine. Whoever was trying to cause harm had run away. I bet they saw one big bad angel standing there saying, "Not this house!" Karen and I have made up our minds to be givers in every possible way. We love blessing others. Sure, we have gone through tough times, but there is something powerful about knowing we were faithful to give. Winston Churchill once said, "We make a living by what we get, and a life by what we give!"[8] I couldn't have said it better myself.

2. We will walk in wisdom.

The devil is referred to as the devourer in Malachi 3:11, and God has called us to be on the alert for him. First Peter 5:8 warns us, "Be self-controlled and alert. Your enemy the devil prowls around like a roaring lion looking for someone to devour." The way to walk in wisdom and guard against the attacks of the enemy on our finances is to follow the rule of "ask, seek, knock" outlined in Matthew 7:8. "For everyone who asks receives; he who seeks finds; and to him who knocks, the door will be opened."

In other words, every opportunity is not a God opportunity. Take a moment to ask God questions concerning your finances and other decisions. If you are married, take time to pray with your spouse about the decisions that need to be made. God will give you wisdom to make the right call. Wisdom means praying for God's will and not your own.

When we seek out wisdom, we begin to distinguish between what we want and what we need. If we live according to our wants, we will forever be playing catch up. I love this prayer in Psalm 119:33–40: "God, teach me lessons for living so I can stay the course. Give me insight so I can do what you tell me—my whole life one long, obedient response. Guide me down the road of your commandments; I love traveling this freeway! Give me a bent for your words of wisdom, and not for piling up loot. Divert my eyes from toys and trinkets, invigorate me on the pilgrim way. Affirm your promises to me—promises made to all who fear you. Deflect the harsh words of my critics—but what you say is always so good. See how hungry I am for your counsel; preserve my life through your righteous ways!" (THE MESSAGE).

My favorite part is where it says, "Divert my eyes from toys and trinkets." Karen has prayed since she was a little girl for wisdom. I started praying for wisdom because I learned it from her. In the early years of our marriage we were always broke financially. Yet when I began to pray for wisdom, it changed everything. God began to shed light on undisciplined areas in my life that I need to change.

Have you ever met people who are always out of money and always needing help to deal with an emergency? They live under the "tyranny of urgent." The Bible speaks of people who have holes in their pockets in Haggai 1:6. "You have planted much, but have harvested little. You eat, but never have enough. You drink, but never have your fill. You put on clothes, but are not warm. You earn wages, only to put them in a purse with holes in it."

No matter how much some people get, they seem to always be in need. This is usually because they never learned to walk in wisdom. They will blame God, their families, their jobs, their past, or whatever seems to be the easiest target, when the real problem is that they simply need to pray for wisdom.

3. We will develop right habits.

Proverbs 18:9 says, "Slack habits and sloppy work are as bad as vandalism" (THE MESSAGE). I honestly believe that a person's future is in his daily routine. My wife and I decided to take the time to be in the know, to study what successful people have done to get there. It is important to develop good habits. Reading leadership materials, going to classes, and asking others to mentor you are all good habits to establish.

One right habit that can help stabilize your finances is to establish a spending limit when you shop. Never buy on a whim. You can use the envelope system and set aside a certain amount in labeled envelopes for your bills, expenses, and other needs. Then you live off of what is left over. Believe it or not, God can't stand it when you're deep in debt because that forces you to live in vice grip of worry and fear.

This is why God said in Matthew 6:30–33: "If God gives such attention to the appearance of wildflowers—most of which are never even seen—don't you think he'll attend to you, take pride in you, do his best for you? What I'm trying to do here is to get you to relax, to not be so preoccupied with getting, so you can respond to God's giving. People who don't know God and the way he works fuss over these things, but you know both God and how he works. Steep your life in God-reality, God-initiative, God-provisions. Don't worry about missing out. You'll find all your everyday human concerns will be met" (THE MESSAGE).

THE BLESSING OF HARD WORK

No discussion about money would be complete without broaching the subject of work. God expects us all to have a healthy work ethic. That means we are to work hard. I encourage you to grab hold of an entrepreneurial spirit. I believe God will give you supernatural ideas and a wisdom-inspired plan to execute those ideas. But there are no short-cuts. Nobody gets ahead without working hard.

Look at what Proverbs says about this: "One day I walked by the field of an old lazybones, and then passed the vineyard of a lout; they were overgrown with weeds, thick with thistles, all the fences broken down. I took a long look and pondered what I saw; the fields preached me a sermon and I listened: 'A nap here, a nap there, a day off here, a day off there, sit back, take it easy—do you know what comes next? Just this: You can look forward to a dirt-poor life, with poverty as your permanent houseguest!'" (Prov. 24:30–31, THE MESSAGE).

Please understand that none of what I have shared is a quick fix, but I want you to see that God is there for you. He wants you to be blessed. In fact, His Word even says He has given us an inheritance. My father was very ill recently after suffering several mild heart attacks and a stroke. He first got sick while on a flight to minister in Africa, so it truly is a miracle that he is still alive today.

Thankfully, my father has regained much of his health, but I will never forget a call I received from him one day while he was still recovering. My dad wanted desperately to meet with my brother and me. He said it was quite urgent. When we arrived the next day to meet with him, he seemed very focused. He began to talk with us about his mortality. This was a conversation my brother and I certainly did not want to have, but Dad was persistent and said, "Boys, this conversation is a must!"

He went on to tell us about provisions he had made should he pass away. He said he had saved enough money to take care of my mom and provide us with a modest inheritance. I remember saying, "Dad, that doesn't matter to us," but that didn't sit well with him. He said, "Son, a good father always leaves an inheritance for his children." That is the absolute truth. Now, that inheritance may not be earthly finances. It may be a good family name or a godly spiritual heritage, but it is a father's duty to provide the inheritance.

Did you know that our heavenly Father has thought about your spiritual inheritance too? You're a rich kid! Your Dad loves you enough to have prepared for your future. First Peter 1:3–5 says, "What a God we have! And how fortunate we are to have him, this Father of our Master Jesus! Because Jesus was raised from the dead, we've been given a brand-new life

and have everything to live for, including a future in heaven—
and the future starts now! God is keeping careful watch over
us and the future. The Day is coming when you'll have it all—
life healed and whole" (THE MESSAGE). We have a lot to look
forward to, no matter what condition our finances are in now.
God wants us to prosper and be blessed, and He is making
provision for us. We just need to trust Him, acknowledge
Him, and walk in obedience.

Chapter 13

GOD IS CHEERING FOR US

L AST YEAR MY daughter, Abby, was taking ice skating lessons. It turned out that Abby was very good at ice skating, and she progressed quickly in the course. One day Abby's coach surprised her by saying that if she wanted to take the test to move up to the next level, she could do so at the end of practice that day. This was a big deal because every student must pass certain tests in order to graduate to the next class. Abby definitely wanted to move forward. The problem was that I was out of town on a ministry trip.

Abby immediately told her coach, "I can't do that today because my daddy is out of town!" The teacher was shocked at her answer but told her, "OK, we will wait till next week." The next week I was able to watch her pass her test. When she finished all of her ice skating moves for the coach, she immediately looked into the stands to see my response. I, of course, stood and clapped and shouted for her. She smiled from ear to ear. Abby wasn't about to go to the next level without her daddy there to cheer her on.

Everyone wants someone to cheer him on in life. We all want to know there is someone who believes in us and is in our corner during the good times and bad. It took me years to realize it, but God is cheering us on. Don't believe me? Look at Zephaniah 3:17: "The Lord your God is in the midst of you, a Mighty One, a Savior [Who saves]! He will rejoice over you with joy; He will rest [in silent satisfaction] and in His love He will be silent and make no mention [of past sins, or even recall them]; He will exult over you with singing" (AMP).

This verse reveals so much about the heart of God our Father. It declares that He is with us, dances over us with joy, and has a selective memory (*whew!*). But my favorite part is the line, "He will rest [in silent satisfaction]." The thought that God rests in silent satisfaction when He thinks about me blows my mind.

It took me years to realize that God actually likes me and believes in me. Embracing that truth required me to completely shift my thinking. I had always seen God as loving but rarely did I see Him as a personal God. In my journey to know God, that changed, and I began to realize that He is my friend and loves me more than I can imagine. God desires relationship with us on every level. He loves it when we talk with Him and get real with Him. He doesn't sit on His throne just waiting to pass judgment on us; rather, He desires to be our friend.

God created you from the inside out (Ps. 139) and took special care with you because He made you for a specific purpose. You are not a mistake but someone God made because He wants to do life with you. He is a God of relationship. He loves you so much you can never get away from Him. He is always knocking on the door of your heart, calling out to you.

I want to go deeper in examining what Zephaniah meant by "silent satisfaction," but first let me explain a little more about who God is. Did you know that God gets excited for you? In fact, He gave you a cheerleader in the Holy Spirit, who "will never leave you" (John 14:16, NLT). Some passages of Scripture refer to the Holy Spirit as a comforter, but I like the word the New Living Translation uses for the Holy Spirit in John 14:16. He is called our "Advocate." I believe there is a special reason this word was chosen. In a blog posting, Father

Ron Shirley offers some important insight into the word *advocate*, which means "counselor" or "gift."

> If you study the word *advocate*, or *gift*, it is the Greek word "Paraclete." That sounds like an odd word until you break down its meaning. "Paraclete" is a Greek word, and the "clete" part of it means to call out or yell. The "para" means vigorously. So "paraclete" means to call out vigorously. Now in some Bibles the word *paraclete* is translated into advocate or consoler. Those words are good, but somewhat churchy and really not earthy, the way that paraclete is in the original language. I think the closest English word we have for paraclete is "cheerleader."[1]

God is not just your Father, friend, and Savior—He is also your cheerleader! I think that is amazing. The Creator of the universe is shouting from the stands of heaven for you—because He is a good Father.

As a dad I realized a long time ago that it is critical for my children to hear and see me at their sporting events, plays, and in other big moments. My son is all grown up now, and I can't believe how fast the time flew by. From the time Nate was just a little boy until he was in junior high school, I was usually his coach during basketball, soccer, football, and baseball seasons. As he would run down the field or court, I would hold my fist high in the air to show that I was cheering him on. Through the years it became our sign to each other.

Several years ago Nate and I had a very serious conversation. We have since come to call it our "August 9 Park Bench Experience." On this particular day I had stopped by to watch his summer football practice, and Nate's coach asked to meet with me. The coach told me that Nate didn't seem to have his heart in playing football. At the time Nate was smaller than the other boys and not quite as athletic as some. So that day while sitting on the park bench with him, I asked Nate what was causing him to lack motivation.

Nate began to tell me that he needed me to be home more and that he felt I was too busy for him. My absence from our home had caused him to lose heart. That was a wake-up call to me, and it caused me to reevaluate how I was managing my time. We both wept that day, and we made a covenant to make our family our top priority.

Something else happened during the "Park Bench Experience." As Nate and I met, I felt God telling me that Nate would receive football scholarship offers from across the nation if he would work hard. I told Nate what I felt God was saying to me. It excited him, but he also knew he would have to work very hard. Over the next few years I would remind him of that day on the park bench and the promise God had given him. He trained constantly and worked hard at football. Eventually he gained body size, speed, and strength, and became a very good football player.

By the time he reached his junior year in high school, he had started for his junior varsity teams two years in a row in the position of nose guard. Then he started playing nose guard on the varsity team of a large 6A high school in Trussville, Alabama, that was known to be an athletics powerhouse. There were several seniors in Nate's position on defense, and the coach believed seniority was most important. So as a junior, Nate got very little playing time on the field.

After games he would come home discouraged because he had barely played. I would tell him to hold on and wait for his moment to arrive. During those games Nate would stand quietly on the sidelines just praying to get into the game. As I watched from the stands, I would hold my fist in the air and scream things such as, "Nate, you're doing great!" Nate would look at me as if I was crazy. He would mouth the words, "Dad, I am not even playing!" The coaches and players thought I was crazy too, but I knew he needed to hear me.

I was always amazed that Nate could hear my voice over the thousands of screaming fans, but I wouldn't put it past God to have tuned Nate's ear to hear my shouts. You see, I knew my son needed to hear my voice during his time of disappointment. A dear friend of mine named Galen Woodward made a deep impact on me years ago when I went to speak at his church in Albuquerque, New Mexico. He missed the service I was speaking at because his son had a football game. Galen knew his son needed to see him cheering. He had his priorities right, and he taught me to make sure mine were in order too. After that I made sure I was there to cheer for my children.

Finally, Nate's senior year began, and it was a banner football season. He earned the starting position for his team and became a defensive force, making tackles, blocks, and sacks. His time had arrived, and he was ready. College coaches from all over the nation began to call our home wanting Nate to play football for their colleges. What God had shared with me back in the summer of Nate's freshman year was now actually happening. Nate even earned the honor of being named defensive player of the year for the state of Alabama.

Nate would eventually accept a football scholarship at a college in Dallas, Texas, just as I had prophesied to him. Even when he was playing for his college team, when the public announcer would call out his name after a great play, he would run off the field holding his fist up to me and smiling. I would stand there with a smile on my face too and my fist held high! I was no longer shouting for him, because I didn't need to do that anymore. He was in the game. He needed me to simply stand there, as Zephaniah 3:17 says, "in silent satisfaction!"

I shared that story to paint a picture of the kind of Father you have. He is cheering for you. He is standing in your midst today, and He is smiling as He takes silent satisfaction in you. He has His fist held high! If you have not heard from God in a while, it is because you are in the game. He is silently cheering you on. He had to scream for you when you were on the sidelines, but now you are in the game!

God believes in you! He wants you to succeed. He takes joy in the prosperity of His children. Just look up and you will see God the Father smiling. He is proud of you. Now don't give up. Remember the promise you've been given in the Book of Isaiah: "Do you not know? Have you not heard? The LORD is the everlasting God, the Creator of the ends of the earth. He will not grow tired or weary, and his understanding no one can fathom. He gives strength to the weary and increases the power of the weak. Even youths grow tired and weary, and young men stumble and fall; but those who hope in the LORD will renew their strength. They will soar on wings like eagles; they will run and not grow weary, they will walk and not be faint" (Isa. 40:28-31).

Now that we have established who your heavenly Father truly is, let's examine some more reasons so many people believe God is mad at them.

PART 3

BUT GOD MUST BE MAD AT ME...

Chapter 14

TERRIBLE THINGS HAVE HAPPENED TO ME

I F GOD IS really good, how can He allow such terrible things to happen?" I have heard that question so many times. One of the first instances was back when I was in sixth grade. My science teacher asked us, "If God is so good, then why are children harmed, women abused, and people hurting?" Those were the last words I expected to hear when I made my first attempt at telling someone about the love of God. My teacher had been dealt some tough blows in life, and back then I was young and simply unprepared to answer her question. But in this chapter I want to address that question for everyone out there like my former science teacher.

It is so easy for us to allow our pain to create our theology. We think if God allows something bad to happen to one of His people, then He must be mad at that person. After all, if we live by faith and walk in obedience, doesn't that mean everything will be perfect? Quite the contrary; Jesus said times would get tough. He said, "I have told you all this so that you may have peace in me. Here on earth you will have many trials and sorrows. But take heart, because I have overcome the world" (John 16:33, NLT).

I can't say I look forward to the trials of life, but I love the promise Jesus gave at the end of the verse: "I have overcome the world." I know sometimes it can feel as if the world is over-coming us. That is when many people begin to think God must be mad at them, but we have to remember that Jesus has over-come the world. God has given us a promise in Psalm 34:19: "A righteous man may have many troubles, but the LORD delivers him from them all."

My knees were weak as I stood there holding the phone. It was five in the morning on August 12, 2007. Just the night before I had flown home from speaking at a conference in California where we saw thousands of lives touched. I was still half asleep when I hung up the phone with tears rolling down my face. I could barely believe what my father had told me. My sister had died in her sleep earlier that morning. My head was spinning. Could this actually be happening?

I raced to the hospital, which was an hour away, thinking the whole time, "Where are You, God? How could You let this happen?" My sister and I were very close, partly because she was only a year and nine months older than me, so we had experienced a lot together in our childhood. During her late teens she walked away from her Christian upbringing and entered a life of misery. Her body was simply exhausted from years of illness and substance abuse. Yet my first reaction as I drove to the hospital was, "God, how could You allow this? I preach Your Word! I have dedicated my life to Your message, Lord. My parents have served You for decades. They don't deserve this. My brother preaches Your Word." I must admit, for a moment I walked in doubt, hurt, and even anger.

I knew my sister's history, and I knew it was a miracle she had lived to the ripe old age of thirty-nine considering all she had been involved in for the last two decades of her life. Yet her death would take me on a six-month journey of deep reflection that would eventually lead me to write this book. As I previously said, my sister had given her heart to Christ four weeks earlier, so I knew she was experiencing heaven and was in the incredible presence of a loving and awesome God. But her family back on earth was living out a nightmare.

I can tell you now what I didn't quite realize then—that my sister didn't die because God was judging or mocking my family, or because He had abandoned us. She died because she was a part of this world.

I could tell you countless stories of godly people who experienced tragedies. I think about the pastor I met in Singapore who lost his small son when the boy's school collapsed during an earthquake in China. When this pastor ran to find his son, all he could see was his shoes sticking out from under the rubble. I've never forgotten how that man responded: he fell to his knees and began to worship the Lord. He knew God was good even though his heart was breaking in two.

Tragedy strikes the righteous and the unrighteous. My dear friends Paul Owens, Joel Stockstill, and Forrest Beiser are heroes of mine. They all pastor amazing churches but not without personal struggles. Pastor Paul Owens was out riding motorcycles with friends one day when he hit a guardrail and tragically lost his leg.

Pastor Joel Stockstill leads one of the largest youth ministries in the world. Yet several years ago his young wife, Aimee, died of cancer, and he faces an ongoing battle with a terrible blood disease that has caused him to be on dialysis for life. But Joel stands firm. He has found true love again and continues to be one of the most powerful voices in our nation.

Last there is Forrest Beiser, who leads Glad Tidings Church in San Francisco, California. Forrest is one of the kindest souls I have ever met, and his church is full of people who have overcome tragic circumstances, people who had lost out and made mistakes yet somehow tripped and fell into the arms of a loving Savior. Forrest was a missionary in Africa for years and now suffers from Parkinson's disease, possibly because of the malaria shots he had to take to minister in Africa. I have seen him stand in the pulpit struggling to hold the microphone, yet all he can do is declare the goodness and love of God.

All of these great leaders have continually praised God through their trials. In fact, they say God has never been closer to them than when they walked through their trials. These warriors obviously understand what Isaiah 45:3 means when it says, "I will give you the treasures of darkness, riches stored in secret places, so that you may know that I am the LORD, the God of Israel, who summons you by name."

One of my favorite Christian authors is philosopher and apologist C. S. Lewis. Many know him for the great Chronicles of Narnia series, but his other writings disclose the struggles and trials he faced in his walk as a believer, one of which was losing his young wife to cancer after only three years of marriage.

Lewis was not afraid to acknowledge that unjust things happen to people who serve a loving and just God. In his book *The Problem of Pain* he famously said, "The problem of pain is atheism's most potent weapon against the Christian faith."[1] In other words, atheists could argue that if God were real and loving, He would never allow His creation to experience pain; therefore, He must not exist. In the same way some Christians may feel God must be mad at them if they go through trials and tribulations.

That mind-set reduces God to someone who is uncaring, lethargic, or out of touch, and nothing could be further from the truth. First Peter 4:19 tells us, "If you find life difficult because you're doing what God said, take it in stride. Trust him. He knows what he's doing, and he'll keep on doing it" (THE MESSAGE). God knows what He is doing. He has given us many promises in His Word, but not once did He ever say we would never face tough times. What He did say was that He would always be with us (Heb. 13:5).

I love God's promise in Psalm 91:14–16: "If you'll hold on to me for dear life...I'll get you out of any trouble. I'll give you the best of care if you'll only get to know and trust me. Call me and I'll answer, be at your side in bad times; I'll rescue you, then throw you a party. I'll give you a long life, give you a long drink of salvation!" (THE MESSAGE). If you will just hold on, God will rescue you, throw you a party, and even give you a glass of salvation.

WE LIVE IN A FALLEN WORLD

It is so easy to think God is mad at us when bad things happen. Yet many times we are reaping the consequences of our own decisions. In Genesis 1 there was no sickness, pain, or disease, but when man fell in Genesis 3, the world was turned upside down because of a choice mankind made. God set boundaries in order to protect mankind, but Adam and Eve chose to think they knew what was best. They fell for the devil's lies, and it caused them to lose their perfect residence in the Garden of Eden.

The devil has control over this earth; thus we are in mortal combat at all times with him. Our flesh is subject to the world we live in and, more importantly, the life we choose to live. In other words, if you work with asbestos, you might develop cancer. If you miss a step on a staircase, you might fall and break your leg because of the force of gravity. If you smoke, you are more likely to develop lung problems, including cancer. So many times our pain is simply a consequence of life.

Whether I like it or not, my sister's body responded to a life not lived well. That does not mean God cannot intervene on our behalf, but God is sovereign, and that means He chooses what to do on our behalf. He also allows us to make choices. On the cross Jesus took our sin and punishment and removed the sting of death. The cross opened for us the door to eternal life. John 17:3 tells us, "And this is eternal life: [it means] to know (to perceive, recognize, become acquainted with, and understand) You, the only true and real God, and [likewise] to know Him, Jesus [as the] Christ (the Anointed One, the Messiah), Whom You have sent" (AMP). Knowing God doesn't mean we can tell Him what to do for us. He is sovereign, and we are His creation.

Some people who were raised in a terrible situation may say, "God must have been angry at me; otherwise He wouldn't have allowed me to grow up this way." I know there are so many people who grew up in terrible homes filled with pain and abuse. After we led a service in the northeast corridor of the United States, a fifteen-year-old girl wrote to tell me that during the service she had been able to forgive the man who had molested her for years. She said being released from the anger and resentment allowed her to go deeper in her walk with Christ. That is what I call making up your mind to get free of what tried to destroy you.

I am also reminded of a young man I met in Salt Lake City who told me he had spent the first fifteen years of his life tied up like an animal, and of another young man in Seattle who told me he saw his father kill another man one day when they went hunting. I could tell you thousands of stories that would break your heart. God is not mad at these young men. That is not why they had such traumatic experiences. We live in a fallen world. The devil has free rein, but we must remember that victory still belongs to God.

God wants us to allow what we have been through to move us into a deeper relationship with Him. He can take all of our pain and use it for His glory. Romans 8:20–21 says, "For the creation was subjected to frustration, not by its own choice, but by the will of the one who subjected it, in hope that the creation itself will be liberated from its bondage to decay and brought into the glorious freedom of the children of God."

People can hurt you, churches can hurt you, friends can hurt you, and life can wear you out. We all get tired and weary, and in those times it is so easy to think that you are going through a trial because God is mad at you. I am reminded of an Internet post I read from a person who was under attack from others. He said, "Could it be possible God is mad at me? The reason I ask is because there is no end to the terrible things that happen to me. When my former neighbors were terrorizing me and people tried to help, everything went wrong."[2]

We all walk through seasons of doubt, but we can't give up. We must hold on. There is a powerful set of verses in Romans 8: "Meanwhile, the moment we get tired in the waiting, God's Spirit is right alongside helping us along. If we don't know how or what to pray, it doesn't matter. He does our praying in and for us, making prayer out of our wordless sighs, our aching groans. He knows us far better than we know ourselves, knows our pregnant condition, and keeps us present before God. That's why we can be so sure that every detail in our lives of love for God is worked into something good" (vv. 26–28, The Message).

That is truly one of my favorite passages! There have been times when I didn't have words to speak in my despair. I would go to pray, and all I could do was sigh and groan. Guess what? God turned those into a heavenly language. He understood everything I was saying. There are days when your spirit is crying out to God, and it may come out as a sigh or groan. God understands it. In fact, the Bible says He is right there beside you. God will turn your pain into an awesome victory. He will use what you are walking through to birth something great.

God Has a Plan

I believe that what you have been through is a great indication of who you are called to be. This makes me think of the journey our family has walked. My wife, Karen, has shared this testimony at thousands of women's gatherings nationwide. For nearly ten years after our son, Nate, was born, we were unable to have another child. We walked in faith believing for

another baby as we went to various doctors and clinics, but we
could not conceive. Great leaders prayed over us at numerous
gatherings, and many of them spoke prophetic words to
encourage us, but still we were unable to have another baby.

Karen tells how for years she felt that maybe she had done
something wrong and God was mad at her. Then one day
while she was praying, God spoke these words to her, "Karen,
in your despair you have to rescue." That is when God began
to show her that there was a little girl who would be born in a
foreign land who would need a mommy. Karen says she now
realizes what she could not see during her time of pain—that
God had a plan. He wasn't punishing her. He was getting her
ready so she could be entrusted with a great gift named Abby.
He was pushing her to have the courage to rescue a child.

Many times it is in the waiting that we realize God was
actually working it all out for us. Look at this amazing passage in the Book of Psalms.

> God makes everything come out right; he puts victims
> back on their feet. He showed Moses how he went
> about his work, opened up his plans to all Israel. God
> is sheer mercy and grace; not easily angered, he's rich
> in love. He doesn't endlessly nag and scold, nor hold
> grudges forever. He doesn't treat us as our sins deserve,
> nor pay us back in full for our wrongs. As high as
> heaven is over the earth, so strong is his love to those
> who fear him. And as far as sunrise is from sunset, he
> has separated us from our sins. As parents feel for their
> children, God feels for those who fear him. He knows
> us inside and out, keeps in mind that we're made of
> mud. Men and women don't live very long; like wild-
> flowers they spring up and blossom, but a storm snuffs
> them out just as quickly, leaving nothing to show they
> were here. God's love, though, is ever and always, eter-
> nally present to all who fear him, making everything

right for them and their children as they follow his Covenant ways and remember to do whatever he said.

—Psalm 103:6–18, The Message

God will work it all out for you. He will put you back on your feet. The passage in Psalm 103 even says God will fix it not only for you but also for your children. That is called reversing the curse or a next-generation blessing! God isn't mad at you; He has you on His mind. Maybe you are reading this chapter just as life has become a living hell for you. Divorce is at your door, turmoil is in your home, or, even worse, you find yourself closing the casket of loved one. You may be in an intensive care unit sitting next to your precious child who is struggling to defeat the monster called cancer.

The writer of Hebrews said it best when he declared, "Let us hold unswervingly to the hope we profess, for he who promised is faithful" (Heb. 10:23). God is faithful! He is there right beside you in the middle of your struggle, calling out to you. Psalm 34:18 promises us that, "The Lord is close to the brokenhearted and saves those who are crushed in spirit." If you are brokenhearted, He is closer to you now than ever. He will comfort you and be your best friend.

Don't give up! Keep reading this book. I want you to know there is hope in the darkness. Before we go any further, I feel I must share a verse that has kept me in my darkest hours. It says, "Let him who walks in the dark, who has no light, trust in the name of the Lord and rely on his God" (Isa. 50:10). God wants you to trust Him, to know He is reliable no matter what you're going through. God has a greater purpose.

Romans 8:28 says, "And we know that in all things God works for the good of those who love him, who have been called according to his purpose." This scripture declares that no matter what you have been through, God can bring it all together. How does God bring it all together? *Clarke's Commentary on the Bible* states:

It is not said that all things shall work for good, but that συνεργει, they work now in the behalf of him who loveth now, αγαπωσι; for both verbs are in the present tense. All these things work together; while they are working, God's providence is working, his Spirit is working, and they are working Together with him. And whatever troubles, or afflictions, or persecutions may arise, God presses them into their service; and they make a part of the general working, and are caused to contribute to the general good of the person who now loves God, and who is working by faith and love under the influence and operation of the Holy Ghost.[3]

The apostle Paul wrote that we are called according to His *purpose*. What does the word *purpose* mean? It means God has a plan. It means He will use what you have been through to change lives. What you have been through is a great indication of who God has called you to be. God wants to put you on public display. He wants to show the world you have made it.

Clarke's commentary goes on to say the word translated "purpose" in Romans 8:28, which is πρόθεσις, or *prothesis*, "means properly a proposition, or a laying down anything in view of others; and is thus applied to the bread that was laid on the table of show-bread. [See Matt. 12:4; Mark 2:26; and Luke 6:4.] Hence, it means, when applied to the mind, a plan or purpose of mind. It implies that God had a plan, purpose, or intention, in regard to all who became Christians. They are not saved by chance or hap-hazard."[4]

Our pain and suffering have a purpose. Don't ask me to explain your life to you right now; in the long run you will explain it to us. You choose what to do with your pain. Will you allow it to destroy you? Or will you use it to display God's glory as He brings it all together on your behalf?

Your pain has to be "purposed" power. Use it according to

His purpose. I have learned that until you can dance in the place you should have died, you will never understand what it means to overcome your history with "His story" of redemption. God is the best at taking what the devil meant for bad and working it for good! I love the way Romans 8:28 reads in THE MESSAGE: "That's why we can be so sure that every detail in our lives of love for God is worked into something good."

There is a microphone waiting to be handed to you. God wants to put you on public display. He wants you to tell your story of freedom, redemption, and victory! That is what happens when you discover God's purpose for your pain.

I will close this chapter with this thought. When I was talking with Karen about this part of the book, she made this profound statement. She said, "Without pain in our lives it is impossible to have compassion for others." That is so true. Your own pain will give you greater understanding for what others go through.

We live in a fallen world where bad things can happen. God wants you to know that He trusts you with your pain. He wants you to "also glory in tribulations" (Rom. 5:3, NKJV). I pray that you will do just that and reverse the plan of the enemy and use your pain for God's glory!

Chapter 15

GOD MADE A MISTAKE WHEN HE CREATED ME

G OD MESSED UP when He made me!" Those are the very words I heard from a young man in San Francisco during an altar service late one evening. He was struggling with a very deep deception that is becoming more and more prevalent today. He thought that maybe he wasn't manufactured in heaven correctly, that perhaps he was trapped in the wrong body, that God had somehow assigned him the wrong gender. As I poured into that young man the truth about God's love and His perfect plan for men and women, I watched him get free of the lie of the enemy. But I know that for many it is easier to blame God and believe the pervading views about sexual identity than deal with the truth. In this chapter we are going to deal with the truth.

We will spend a lot of time dealing with a major deception that is leaving tremendous hurt and pain in its wake. But I want to be clear that no matter what you struggle with—the family you were born into, the way you look, a learning challenge, or some other issue—you are not a mistake. God made you, and He got it right the first time.

Ephesians 1:11–12 says, "It's in Christ that we find out who we are and what we are living for. Long before we first heard of Christ and got our hopes up, he had his eye on us, had designs on us for glorious living, part of the overall purpose he is working out in everything and everyone" (THE MESSAGE). In this passage the apostle Paul is saying God is the architect of our lives. He has designs for us. None of us are an "oops" or an accident.

You are a marvelous piece of humanity God created in the secret place. Long before you were born, God had plans for you. He destined you for greatness. You are valued and loved by God. He has crazy dreams and visions for you, and no matter what you've done, God has the power to redeem all of your wrongs.

Psalm 139:13–16 paints a picture of how unique you truly are. It says, "Oh yes, you shaped me first inside, then out; you formed me in my mother's womb. I thank you, High God— you're breathtaking! Body and soul, I am marvelously made! I worship in adoration—what a creation! You know me inside and out, you know every bone in my body; you know exactly how I was made, bit by bit, how I was sculpted from nothing into something. Like an open book, you watched me grow from conception to birth; all the stages of my life were spread out before you, the days of my life all prepared before I'd even lived one day" (THE MESSAGE).

You see, God doesn't make mistakes. He knows who and what He has made. He celebrated when you were born. He has plans for you. You're made in His image (Gen. 1:27), and He likes what He made!

IT'S OK TO NOT FIT IN

As I said previously, we live in a fallen world, a world where culture collides with reality and biblical truth often stands in opposition to its belief system. The apostle Paul warned us in Romans 12:2 to be very careful to recognize our surroundings. He said, "Don't become so well-adjusted to your culture that you fit into it without even thinking. Instead, fix your attention on God. You'll be changed from the inside out. Readily recognize what he wants from you, and quickly respond to it. Unlike the culture around you, always dragging you down to its level of immaturity, God brings the best out of you, develops well-formed maturity in you" (THE MESSAGE).

God wants His best for you, but the devil loves to send confusion into young lives, especially in the area of sexuality. Because the world teaches that just about any and everything goes when it comes to sexual expression, many people think their Maker is to blame when someone desires things that are contrary to God's Word. The Bible is clear about the dangers of questioning God. Romans 9:20–21 says, "But who are you, O man, to talk back to God? 'Shall what is formed say to him who formed it, "Why did you make me like this?"' Does not the potter have the right to make out of the same lump of clay some pottery for noble purposes and some for common use?"

The world says all kinds of things are OK. It says a person can be in the wrong body, that someone who is physically male can be female inside and vice versa. It will question God's ability to get a person's gender right the first time. But God doesn't make mistakes. It is simply not true that a person can be born in the wrong body. This is really a sign of the spiritual battle being waged all around us. Paul said be aware of the culture around you!

In February 2011 pop star Lady Gaga released a song called "Born This Way." She sings that God made her the way she is, and that she is beautiful because God doesn't make mistakes. It sounds great, right? But remember, our culture is at war with the truth. In the same song Lady Gaga goes on to say it's not a sin to have a different kind of lover. She tells her listeners not to be a drag but to be queens, because God makes no mistakes.

Does something in you say, "No, she is wrong"? The song may have sounded good at first, but soon it becomes clear that Lady Gaga is justifying—celebrating—any kind of lifestyle in the name of God. She is declaring, "Don't fight it! You were born this way." She is essentially saying you can live any way you want because God made you the way you are. The devil is a liar, and he loves to misconstrue the truth. I will show you later in this book just how much the devil is liar!

Whenever I hear Lady Gaga's song, I want to replace it with another song I know. It is a worship song called "I Know Who I Am" by Israel Houghton and New Breed. He says he knows who he is—he belongs to Jesus! He is healed, secure, forgiven, accepted—all because Christ is his identity! Those words are life!

In today's culture there are always forces pitting us between opinion and truth. This can lead to cognitive dissonance. That is an uncomfortable feeling people experience when they attempt to believe two contradictory ideas at the same time. When two attitudes, beliefs, facts, or behaviors are in conflict, people are driven to reduce the dissonance by changing their existing attitudes or beliefs, adding new ones to create consistency, or by reducing the importance of one of the ideas in conflict.[1] In other words, you can want to believe something so badly that you change what you know to be true in order to get rid of the "dissonance" making you feel uncomfortable.

This is happening now more than ever in the area of sexuality. From America's largest corporations sponsoring gay pride parades to the Lutheran Church ordaining gay and lesbian ministers[2] or Ben and Jerry's Vermont ice cream company naming one of their flavors "Hubby Hubby"[3] in honor of gay marriage, the culture is screaming loudly, telling us what we should believe. Instead of resisting the tide of popular opinion, so many are simply changing their views to fit what the culture says is true.

The push to change America's views about sexuality is not only coming from businesses and churches but also from our government leaders. Each year the president of the United States awards the Medal of Freedom to individuals who have made "meritorious contribution to the security or national interests of the United States, world peace, cultural or other significant public or private endeavors."[4] It is the highest civilian award given in the United States. Check out who the 2009 class of recipients included:

1. Harvey Milk, the first openly homosexual San Francisco politician

2. Billie Jean King, the tennis star of the 1960s and 1970s who made headlines for declaring herself a lesbian in 1981, for having helped "champion gender equality issues not only in sports, but in all areas of public life"

3. South African Anglican Archbishop Desmond Tutu, one of the leading promoters of homosexual sin among African prelates in the Anglican Church[5]

It's no secret that the homosexual agenda has admirers in the highest office in the land. During a press conference last year President Barack Obama said, "This administration, under my direction, has consistently said we cannot discriminate as a country against people on the basis of sexual orientation. And we have done more in the two and a half years that I've been in here than the previous forty-three presidents to uphold that principle."[6] In fact, on May 9, 2012, while being interviewed by Robin Roberts, President Obama declared that he had evolved on the issue of gay marriage. Here are his words: "I have to tell you that over the course of several years as I have talked to friends and family and neighbors when I think about members of my own staff who are in incredibly committed monogamous relationships, same-sex relationships, who are raising kids together, when I think about those soldiers or airmen or Marines or sailors who are out there fighting on my behalf and yet feel constrained, even now that

Don't Ask Don't Tell is gone, because they are not able to commit themselves in a marriage, at a certain point I've just concluded that for me personally it is important for me to go ahead and affirm that I think same-sex couples should be able to get married."[7]

With so many voices affirming homosexuality, it's easy to see why there is confusion in this generation. A different message must be proclaimed. Is homosexuality wrong? The apostle Paul said in 1 Corinthians 6:9, "Do you not know that the unrighteous and the wrongdoers will not inherit or have any share in the kingdom of God? Do not be deceived (misled): neither the impure and immoral, nor idolaters, nor adulterers, nor those who participate in homosexuality" (AMP).

Is homosexuality wrong? Yes, it is wrong! The Bible says it is sin. I know that is not politically correct to say, but truth is rarely politically correct. The fact of the matter is any kind of sin is going to do its best to destroy us. And it is our responsibility as Christians to warn people that sin is really out to kill, steal, and destroy their lives. The problem is that in the Christian world we have preached that certain sins are worse than others. As a result, people have come to hate Bible-believing Christians, the very ones God wants to use to get His message out. Our mission is not to condemn one group of people, but to love all people and show everyone the redeeming power of God and His awesome love. We must present the truth but always in a loving and honorable way.

GOD CAN FILL OUR DEEPEST LONGING

Many have come to believe it is impossible for people to be freed of same-sex attraction, but all over the nation I have seen students and adults discover their true identities through Christ. I received this testimony from a teenage girl not long ago: "God freed me from my mental oppression. My chains are freed. The idea of homosexuality was burned from my memory. I am free from the lies that I let seep into my heart. God revealed new pieces of my calling." God is able to break any chain. He is not powerless in the face of homosexuality or any other sin, no matter what the world says.

I recently had the incredible honor of speaking at the National Youth Leaders Conference in Atlanta, Georgia. This amazing event is hosted biannually by Pastor Jeanne Mayo. This is always a powerful conference, and I personally was looking forward to hearing one of the speakers, a man by the name of Sy Rogers. I had heard a great deal about Sy from friends in ministry who had been blessed by his ministry. Sy has an amazing testimony of redemption out of the homosexual lifestyle. He has now been in ministry for more than thirty years and has a beautiful family.

During his session I sat with expectation to hear this great leader share his victory through Christ out of a life of despair and hurt. As I listened to him, I was overwhelmed with compassion for those who fight the war for truth concerning sexuality, as well as for those embroiled in the lies of the enemy. Sy acknowledged that everyone has failings that keep them from experiencing God's best, and he was quick to share that God can redeem anyone from any lifestyle.[8] After all, Jesus Himself came from the lineage of Rahab the harlot.

This generation longs to be loved, and Sy said that for many people, "Bad love is better than no love at all."[9] Like all people throughout history, this generation has an insatiable hunger for love and companionship. In fact, people are so hungry to be loved they settle for anything that feeds their flesh. It is the hunger games! I am, of course, referring to the first book in the trilogy written by Suzanne Collins. This series depicts a fictitious culture of postwar rebels who are willing to play in a real game of chance and battle one another to receive a lifetime of food. The heroes and villains fight to the end just to know they will have another meal.

The books are wildly popular, and so is the first film in the trilogy. In fact, the movie remained at the number one spot in the box office for four weeks straight.[10] Why? Because I believe the story speaks to the hunger in our culture. People are looking for something that satisfies, but they don't know what they truly want. The Bible talks about what happens when people are willing to satisfy their hunger with anything. "He who is full loathes honey, but to the hungry even what is bitter tastes sweet" (Prov. 27:7).

God can gratify our deepest hunger. He knows exactly what we want, and He can give it to us. So when our flesh screams for a meal filled with lust, we must make up our minds to trust that God has something better waiting for us, a life filled with love and purpose. Psalm 107:8–9 says God "satisfies the thirsty and fills the hungry with good things." Jesus also promised in Matthew 5:6 that in the end we would be filled if we hunger and thirst for His righteousness.

SHARE THE TRUTH WITH LOVE AND RESPECT

Christians are losing the cultural war for truth concerning sexuality and gender reconciliation. One reason is that in our desire to minister to homosexuals, many well-intentioned Christian leaders and churches have not shown respect or wisdom toward those grappling with these issues. We have shown so much disdain for the gay lifestyle that we have given ammunition to those who claim we are filled with hate toward homosexuals. In the end we play right into the hands of those who would love to discredit our message. The call to live holy is not a weapon to use against people who need to know the power of God's love. We must respect every individual as part of God's creation instead of hurling insults.

I believe that every person is created with a deep longing for revelation and truth. Therefore, we must bring truth with love and honor. What if we began our conversations with homosexuals by saying, "I deeply care about you and desire to help you discover God's plan for your life"? I believe if we approached people with warmth and kindness that comes directly from the heart of Jesus, they may be more open to receiving our message. We must not make it our goal to win an argument but rather to share the love of God.

At his session in Atlanta, Sy Rogers said, "Rules and rituals will never save you, but relationship without condemnation is transformational."[11] As Christians we know it is the goodness of God that transforms a person (Rom. 2:4). So we must allow God's Spirit to do the work of changing people. He is much better at it than we are. After all, He is the one who knit each of us together.

God is not anti-fun; He doesn't want us to hurt ourselves. God will forgive, but biology doesn't. The sin we commit against our bodies doesn't go away. Whether it's overeating or engaging in sexual sin, there are consequences for going beyond the boundaries God set for our bodies. As Christians we must share this truth because we have the individual's best interests at heart, not because we want to advance an agenda.

It is my heart's desire to share truth and not opinion. The fact is that we are not born gay, but we can be influenced by our surroundings. That is why it is critical for parents or guardians to do their best to protect children from the corruption that is so prevalent on television, the Internet, and other forms of media. It's shocking to believe, but there are children who regularly view pornography. As Sy Rogers said, "This is generation XXXX! We must have prevention and not repair!"[12]

Many times our sexual orientation comes from our history. If that history includes abuse, abandonment, or mistreatment, then love may be more easily accepted from those who seem safe, even if that is a person of the same gender. It must be the goal of today's Christian leaders to help this hurting generation heal from past abuses. We live in a fallen world where horrible things happen, and we cannot allow ourselves to be defined by what took place in the past. Only through Christ will we ever find our true identities. All of us have to push past the labels that have been placed upon us since childhood and discover the true God DNA that lies within us.

As I have said before, it is not my desire to see anyone hurting or in pain. This is why I must share the truth about homosexuality. I do so in love, but also with science. Here are some facts about homosexuality:

- Procreation cannot take place without a man and a woman.

- There are no replicated scientific studies supporting any specific biological cause for homosexuality.[13]

- Laws and moral standards are not set in place based on feelings. God's principles must be the foundation for our laws and moral standards. Therefore marriage is defined and sanctified by God's law, not human preference.[14]

- In several studies gay and bisexual men were three times as likely to report having been sexually abused as children as heterosexual men.[15]

- Gay and bisexual men are more severely affected by homosexuality than any other group. In 2009 they accounted for 61 percent of all new HIV infections and 49 percent of people living with HIV.[16]

- Sexually transmitted diseases are increasing among homosexuals, putting those involved in the gay lifestyle at greater risk of infection.[17]

Now that we understand the facts, let me tell you the truth about homosexuality.

- The truth is, homosexuals can be set free. Many are angry and wounded, and the last thing they need is to be judged by self-righteous church-goers. That is why Christians must walk in love, truth, and the power of the Holy Spirit when ministering to homosexuals.

- Fathers play the greatest role in teaching true biblical sexuality to a child. So unless the tide shifts and the hearts of the fathers turn back toward their children, we will continue to see a generation confused about their identity and their worth.

- We cannot accept the cultural pressure to reason with sin. God does not make mistakes. He would not create a person to be something He has commanded him not to be. A homosexual can discover his true identity in Christ and be completely restored. But he must desire to be free.

God has raised up some wonderful ministries for those battling unwanted same-sex attraction. Groups such as Exodus International (www.exodusinternational.org) and Homosexual Anonymous Fellowship (www.ha-fs.org) offer amazing counseling programs led by people who themselves have experienced freedom from the homosexual lifestyle. As Christians we may not have all the answers, but if we return to love without reason and holiness without compromise, we can help guide those searching for answers to the source of all truth.

I am sharing all of this because misinformation seems to be one of the biggest reasons people believe God must have somehow created them incorrectly. God can set anyone free. His arm is long enough to reach the most challenging situation. Isaiah 59:1–2 says, "Look! Listen! God's arm is not

amputated—he can still save. God's ears are not stopped up—
he can still hear" (THE MESSAGE). Not only can God reach
you, but He can also hear you!

You were born to be a champion for God. He has called
you and me to live holy lives separate from the world. God
doesn't want us to suffer the fruit of bad choices when He
has better plans for us. Look at what the apostle Paul said
in 1 Corinthians 15:34: "Think straight. Awaken to the holiness of life. No more playing fast and loose with resurrection
facts. Ignorance of God is a luxury you can't afford in times
like these. Aren't you embarrassed that you've let this kind of
thing go on as long as you have?" (THE MESSAGE).

GOD GOT IT RIGHT THE FIRST TIME

As I mentioned at the beginning of this chapter, there are
other things in life besides sexual identity that rob us of our
confidence that God made us perfectly the first time. If you
don't think you're the brightest or best looking, or if your
stature or girth make you feel less than your peers, it may
be easy to think you were somehow shortchanged in the creation process. But you are as Psalm 139:14 says, "fearfully and
wonderfully made." That's right—you were made for a purpose! Ephesians 2:10 says, "We are God's handiwork, created
in Christ Jesus to do good works, which God prepared in
advance for us to do" (NIV, 2011).

The word "handiwork," or "workmanship," in the Greek
is *poiēma*, which is the same word translated poem, song, or
something created in unique fashion.[18] In other words, you
are God's song to the world, His expression of love and victory! He knew what He was doing when He made you. You
are not illegitimate; your Father knows you. You have been
created with a destiny.

I know I have a lot of favorite scriptures, but one of my all-
time favorite verses is Jeremiah 29:11. It says, "'For I know the

plans I have for you,' declares the LORD, 'plans to prosper you and not to harm you, plans to give you hope and a future.'" When my son was just a baby, I put that scripture over his bed. I have also shared that verse over and over with my daughter. I love to remind her how special she truly is to our family.

God has all of us in His sight. Did you know you are even engraved on His hand? God has a tattoo of you! Isaiah 49:15–16 says, "Can a mother forget the baby at her breast and have no compassion on the child she has borne? Though she may forget, I will not forget you! See, I have engraved you on the palms of my hands; your walls are ever before me." Our names are written on the giant hand of God. Every time He reaches out to rescue you, He sees your name!

In my early years there were times when I just didn't feel I could do anything right. I can remember having deep talks with my dad and him telling me, "Son, God don't make no junk!" God has been planning, waiting, and watching as your life has unfolded. He created you with gifts no one else has. Did you know that you have four distinct attributes unlike anyone else? You have a unique eye print, fingerprint, tongue print, and Helix DNA. In other words, you are the only one who sees what you are called to see, touches whom you are called to touch, and speaks the words you are called to speak—and you have a God print!

I believe with all my heart that in this day and time you must draw a line in the sand. You must guard what you hear, say, and believe. The enemy loves to sow seeds of confusion. But God has given us a powerful promise in Jude: "But you, dear friends, carefully build yourselves up in this most holy faith by praying in the Holy Spirit, staying right at the center of God's love, keeping your arms open and outstretched, ready for the mercy of our Master, Jesus Christ. This is the unending life, the real life!" (v. 20, THE MESSAGE).

I love the last part of that verse—this is "the real life!" When you trust God with who you are, He will move you from the fantasy others have created about you into the reality of who He made you to be.

I believe one of the greatest roles spiritual leaders play is that of a spiritual parent. God will bring leaders or spiritual parents into our lives to teach us discipline, identity, and purpose, and to help bring direction. In 2 Timothy the apostle Paul guides his spiritual son Timothy and reminds him of his purpose. It is most likely that God used the apostle Paul to bring Timothy's family to Christ. We know that Timothy had a great spiritual heritage because Paul says in 2 Timothy 1:5, "I am reminded of your sincere faith, which first lived in your grandmother Lois and in your mother Eunice and, I am persuaded, now lives in you also."

The Bible tells us in Acts 16:1 that Timothy's father was a Greek who had no relationship with Christ. That lets us know that Timothy probably did not gain a strong sense of identity from his father. A father has the power to declare his child's identity. Timothy didn't have anyone to do that for him spiritually until the apostle Paul came along and became his spiritual father.

The apostle Paul goes on to tell Timothy, "For this reason I remind you to fan into flame the gift of God, which is in you through the laying on of my hands. For God did not give us a spirit of timidity, but a spirit of power, of love and of self-discipline. So do not be ashamed to testify about our Lord, or ashamed of me his prisoner" (2 Tim. 1:6–8). In this passage Paul is confronting several issues in Timothy's life, but I believe the biggest one was a spirit of intimidation that comes upon people who do not have a father in their lives. Timothy needed someone to tell him who he was in Christ.

Paul tells Timothy to stir up the fire that is in him, to not be timid or insecure because God has given him His love, power, and a life of discipline. He was being a father to Timothy when he told Timothy to fan the fire that was in him and to be a bold witness for Christ. Timothy had a Christian mother and grandmother, but he needed a father to speak into his life. This spiritual father was validating his son's identity. He was spurring on his disciple. I believe with all my heart that this generation needs to hear who God has called them to be. We must declare it. Remember, it doesn't matter what heritage our earthly father left us; all that matters is what heritage we leave others.

I will close this chapter with something very powerful that Sy Rogers said at the conference in Atlanta. He said he was able to be set free from homosexuality because his church did three things right:

1. *They accepted him.* With their words and their actions they communicated to Sy, "You are so dear to me and so dear to God. He created you with a plan. The world needs what He invested in you, and we would rather have you messy than to not have you at all!"

2. *They offered true accountability.* Sy's church walked with him through his struggles to leave his old way of living, and they never gave up on him. This meant they were intrusive at times. They continually reminded him of the truth of God's Word. God's powerful Word is "sharp as a surgeon's scalpel, cutting through everything, whether doubt or defense, laying us open to listen and obey. Nothing and no one is impervious to God's Word" (Heb. 4:12–13, The Message). By keeping him accountable to the Word of God, Sy's church showed him that they wanted to help him go to another level. They showed him that life without regret is the reward.

3. *They walked with him.* The church walked with
Sy. They rejoiced and grieved beside him. They
never let go of his hand as he discovered truth
in Christ.[19]

Sy Rogers became a man who is unashamed to share his
story and bring healing to the world because he was shown
true love. I want to see the church wrap this generation in its
arms and show them that they are not a mistake. God created
them for a purpose—and He got it right the first time.

Chapter 16

MY CHURCH TEACHES
THAT GOD IS ANGRY

S EVERAL YEARS AGO I was sitting on a long overseas flight reading a book by Joel Osteen, pastor of Lakewood Church in Houston, Texas. While I was reading, a flight attendant sat down beside me and said, "That's my pastor!" I was surprised by how excited she was that Joel Osteen was her pastor. But after she shared her story with me, I began to understand.

She said that she and her husband, who was one of the pilots flying the plane, had been married only a short time. When they met, they both were going through tough divorces. Even though their divorces weren't finalized, they began dating and eventually moved in together.

One night they were watching television and happened upon Pastor Osteen. They heard a message of love and redemption, and it stirred them deeply. They continued to watch his program as often as possible. The flight attendant said Pastor Joel's compassionate and loving message was exactly what she and her husband needed to hear. In time they both realized they were not living the life God had planned for them. They were married a short while later and started attending Lakewood Church regularly.

I had always appreciated Pastor Osteen's ministry, but after meeting this woman I began to truly thank God for him. I realized how powerful positive yet truthful voices could be in reaching this generation with the truth that God loves them. Unfortunately, those kinds of voices are not always easy to find.

When I was growing up, I was constantly told of everything I couldn't do as a Christian. Rarely did I hear of all God had planned for me. In fact, for a while as a teenager I thought serving God was impossible. I felt like a big mess-up. I didn't think I could ever manage to please God. Boy, was I wrong!

You see, God loves relationship, not religion. Religion is man's search for God, but when we accept Christ, we have found Him. It's true that God gives us rules to follow, as I said previously, and those boundaries are for our good. In the best cases these rules are meant to guide us toward the things that please God. But they can easily turn into expectations from people who will judge and condemn us if we fail to tow the line. This has caused tremendous hurt that God never intended. God gave us His Spirit to guide us and help us break free of the sins that bound us before we met Him. And though He uses people to help us grow, He doesn't actually need any help doing His job. Look what God told the people of Israel when they took it upon themselves to decide which laws God wanted mankind to have.

> You say, "The way of the Lord is not just." Hear, O house of Israel: Is my way unjust? Is it not your ways that are unjust? If a righteous man turns from his righteousness and commits sin, he will die for it; because of the sin he has committed he will die. But if a wicked man turns away from the wickedness he has committed and does what is just and right, he will save his life. Because he considers all the offenses he has committed and turns away from them, he will

surely live; he will not die. Yet the house of Israel says,
"The way of the Lord is not just." Are my ways unjust,
O house of Israel? Is it not your ways that are unjust?
                                          —EZEKIEL 18:25–29

Man has always tried to force God to fit his understanding.
And just as the Israelites did, we keep trying to create rules we
think God wants mankind to follow. God gave us His Word
as our road map for life. Those are the rules He wants us to
follow. God's plan is usually the opposite of man's. Proverbs
16:9 says, "In his heart a man plans his course, but the LORD
determines his steps." That's why we should let God's character, and not a particular church or doctrine, set the guidelines for our lives.

So often religious groups, denominations, and/or churches
have created an atmosphere where it seems impossible to be a
faithful Christian. They have developed so many rules it seems
impossible for a believer to feel he has any freedom in Christ.
Religious dos and don'ts will always create an environment for
God's character to be misunderstood. Do we need the law?
Absolutely. The boundaries God set for us in His Word are
critical for us to walk in safety and freedom. He tells us not
to sin against our bodies; not to lie, cheat, or steal; and not to
neglect prayer and worship because this helps us grow closer
to Him, not because He wants us to jump through hoops in
order to please Him.

There are thousands of people who believe God is mad at
them because their church made it impossible for anyone to
please God. Maybe they set strict guidelines for people to
become members or isolated individuals who made mistakes.
I honestly believe many of the people who no longer want
to call themselves Christians never walked away from God—
fellow believers pushed them away from the faith.

WE NEED THE SPIRIT AND THE LAW

Many people equate the law with (bad) rules and the Spirit with (good) freedom. We must realize that both law and Spirit are good. Without laws I wouldn't have so many speeding tickets on my record. You see, the law is there to keep us in line. It protects us from ourselves. Isn't it amazing how many brake lights come on when a police officer is parked along a freeway? The policeman is a reminder that we'd better obey the law.

God's laws help us set boundaries in our lives. I have established boundaries in my life to protect who I have become in Christ. For example, if something comes on television that could harm who I am in Christ, I turn it off. I'm not being a religious person; I'm doing what I need to do to maintain my integrity as a Christian and be a man of honor.

In His Sermon on the Mount Jesus made a promise that the pure in heart will see God (Matt. 5:8). I want to see God, so I have set up boundaries to keep my life pure. The law and Spirit work together. I am very guarded not to allow junk in front of my eyes not only because I want to honor Jesus but also because I honor my wife and children.

I believe God has the power to convict us of sin and lead us to righteousness. Righteous is a fancy word that simply means to be made right in the sight of God. We can be made righteous because Jesus came and abolished the law of sin that once held a grip upon us. Romans 8:2 says that "through Christ Jesus the law of the Spirit of life set me free from the law of sin and death."

Jesus was always at war with the Pharisees and other teachers of the law. Their job was to make sure the people kept the law, but they failed to understand that Jesus had the power to change the law. His coming was a game-changer. The Pharisees were wrapped up in traditions and religious ceremony, and Jesus came to make God personal. Jesus was constantly challenging them for their attitude, and as you'll see in the passage below, He didn't mince words.

> You're hopeless, you religion scholars and Pharisees! Frauds! You keep meticulous account books, tithing on every nickel and dime you get, but on the meat of God's Law, things like fairness and compassion and commitment—the absolute basics!—you carelessly take it or leave it. Careful bookkeeping is commendable, but the basics are required. Do you have any idea how silly you look, writing a life story that's wrong from start to finish, nitpicking over commas and semicolons? You're hopeless, you religion scholars and Pharisees! Frauds! You burnish the surface of your cups and bowls so they sparkle in the sun, while the insides are maggoty with your greed and gluttony. Stupid Pharisee! Scour the insides, and then the gleaming surface will mean something.
> —MATTHEW 23:23–26, THE MESSAGE

I guess you can tell Jesus knew how to make enemies! He was telling them that religious rules won't set a man free, but only through the Spirit of God can a man get rid of whatever has him bound. John 6:63 tells us, "The Spirit gives life; the flesh counts for nothing. The words I have spoken to you are spirit and they are life." And we see in John 4:24 that God is looking for those who will "worship in spirit and in truth"!

We do not live according to the old written code. Romans 7:6 says, "But now, by dying to what once bound us, we have been released from the law so that we serve in the new way of the Spirit, and not in the old way of the written code."

I once heard author John Bevere share a great analogy about the law and the Spirit. He said, "On the straight and narrow path there are two ditches on each side of the road you could drive into. Those two ditches are called Legalism and Lawlessness." Our goal must be to stay on the right path!

It is God's Spirit that convicts us and leads us to righteousness. In the Gospel of John Jesus spoke about the role of the Spirit of God. He said when the Holy Spirit comes, "he will convict the world of guilt in regard to sin and righteousness and judgment" (John 16:8). The Holy Spirit does a great job of changing our hearts. We need anointed pastors and leaders in our lives to help guide us through our walk; that is why Jesus called them shepherds. Sheep need shepherds. But the Holy Spirit is the one who changes our hearts, not people.

Do we need the church? Absolutely. God established the church to be His mouth, hands, and feet. Each of us has a part to play, and when we all come together, we are one body. First Corinthians 12:12 says, "The body is a unit, though it is made up of many parts; and though all its parts are many, they form one body. So it is with Christ."

God has called us to do life together. The church was meant to be a place of refuge and power. It is a place for us to encounter God and have communion with friends. Hebrews 10:25 exhorts believers to never give up "meeting together, as some are in the habit of doing, but...encourage one another— and all the more as you see the Day approaching."

We need one another. We are in a spiritual battle, and there is strength in numbers. That is why we must so be careful of harming one another. The last place you should worry about getting hurt is at your church. When a church has cliques or people who routinely gossip, people get hurt. Churches should be filled with people walking in love, power, and the authority we have as believers in Jesus. I am not saying there is not a place for leaders to bring needed correction within a church. I believe church leaders must deal with issues when they arise. But that kind of correction should flow from a heart of love, not judgment.

WE ARE FREE IN HIM

God has called us to be free in Him. The Bible says where
the Spirit of the Lord is, there is liberty (2 Cor. 3:17). You
are called to live a Spirit-led life. So if you have been hurt
in church, I challenge you to forgive and move forward. The
church needs you, and you need the church. Find a church
that forgives people's pasts and believes the best for their
future. The church isn't a building or pews; it is people who
are called to a great purpose!

I've met many people who are dissatisfied with their
churches. They tell me all that is wrong with the pastor or
the worship team or the youth ministry. Complaining will
accomplish very little. Speak life about your church and its
leadership. If you cannot stand with them, leave, but don't
leave angry. God will lead you to a new church home where
you can grow.

Jesus told a powerful parable about ten virgins in Matthew
25. I believe this story represents the state of the church.

> God's kingdom is like ten young virgins who took
> oil lamps and went out to greet the bridegroom. Five
> were silly and five were smart. The silly virgins took
> lamps, but no extra oil. The smart virgins took jars of
> oil to feed their lamps. The bridegroom didn't show
> up when they expected him, and they all fell asleep.
> In the middle of the night someone yelled out, "He's
> here! The bridegroom's here! Go out and greet him!"
> The ten virgins got up and got their lamps ready. The
> silly virgins said to the smart ones, "Our lamps are
> going out; lend us some of your oil." They answered,
> "There might not be enough to go around; go buy your
> own." They did, but while they were out buying oil,
> the bridegroom arrived. When everyone who was
> there to greet him had gone into the wedding feast,
> the door was locked. Much later, the other virgins,

the silly ones, showed up and knocked on the door, saying, "Master, we're here. Let us in." He answered, "Do I know you? I don't think I know you." So stay alert. You have no idea when he might arrive.

—MATTHEW 25:1-13, THE MESSAGE

Half of the church is ready, and the other half is not. "Ready for what?" you might ask. Ready for God to come and visit the house! The women in the parable were virgins. That means they were pure. But half were focused on greeting the bridegroom and the other half were just playing a game. Half of the virgins wanted to spend time with the Bridegroom, and the other half had allowed their passion for more of God to run dry. That is called living in religion.

All ten virgins were waiting. They were expecting the bridegroom to come at any time. But there is a huge difference between expecting and preparing, and only five of the virgins were prepared. When the bridegroom showed up at the door, the five foolish virgins had no oil. Matthew 25:7–9 says, "The foolish ones said to the wise, 'Give us some of your oil; our lamps are going out.' 'No,' they replied, 'there may not be enough for both us and you. Instead, go to those who sell oil and buy some for yourselves.'"

We must keep the oil in our lamps. The oil represents God's anointing. It represents His Spirit and touch upon our lives. God has anointed you for greatness. You have a great promise in Psalm 23:5–6: "You prepare a table before me in the presence of my enemies. You anoint my head with oil; my cup overflows. Surely goodness and love will follow me all the days of my life, and I will dwell in the house of the LORD forever."

It is a personal goal of mine to always walk in God's anointing. I have learned the anointing is worth everything I have to give up in order to keep it. Remember, you are anointed! Isaiah 61:1–3 tells us: "The Spirit of the Sovereign

Lord is on me, because the Lord has anointed me to preach good news to the poor. He has sent me to bind up the brokenhearted, to proclaim freedom for the captives and release from darkness for the prisoners, to proclaim the year of the Lord's favor and the day of vengeance of our God, to comfort all who mourn, and provide for those who grieve in Zion—to bestow on them a crown of beauty instead of ashes, the oil of gladness instead of mourning, and a garment of praise instead of a spirit of despair."

This passage tells us what God can do for us when His Spirit is upon us. God has given us spiritual gifts, and He expects us to walk in them. (See 1 Corinthians 12; 14.) God has an awesome plan for you, and He has given you exactly what you need to fulfill that plan. You are anointed to do what God created you to accomplish in the first place!

God's heart isn't to have us follow a bunch of rules; He is all about freedom! If religion made you think God was mad at you, I hope and pray you realize that religion got it wrong. Please don't blame God for mankind's mistake.

God's church is still His vehicle for bringing lasting and loving transformation. There are so many powerful churches out there changing lives. I think of Trinity Church near Dallas, Texas, which is led by my dear friend Jim Hennesy. This great church recently purchased an old mansion for the sole purpose of rescuing hurting girls, and it is aptly named "Hope Mansion." There are so many other wonderful churches that I could name.

First, there is Calvary Temple Worship Center in Modesto, California, which is led by Pastor Glen Berteau. This church feeds and clothes thousands through its Nineveh project. And then there's Daystar Family Church in Northport, Alabama, which is led by my brother, Scott Schatzline. This church helped bring healing to a community devastated by the tornadoes that struck the Southeast in April 2011. For weeks they provided thousands of meals, resources, and shelter, and helped to restore lives! This cutting-edge church, known for its large productions and powerful programs for the arts, became a hospital of hope to the weary.

You see, God is not done with the church. He is calling His church outside the four walls to minister hope and love! One ministry called Fresh Start Church has even started having services outside in their community twice a year. Located on the northwest side of Phoenix, Arizona, this powerhouse has the entire congregation meet for worship in the front yard of a dilapidated home, school, or park when it holds these outdoor services, and after church they spend the day cleaning, painting, and restoring the neighbrhood!

I could go on and on. I think of the Church at South Las Vegas, which is led by Pastor Benny Perez. They are touching a hurting city with outreaches that include rescuing and restoring prostitutes. And Calvary Christian Center in Ormond Beach, Florida, where Pastors Jim and Dawn Raley have made it their mission to transform everyone in their city through outreach, feeding the hungry, clothing the poor, giving school supplies to all in need, and transforming lives through every kind of media. The testimonies flowing out of this house on a weekly basis would bring tears to your eyes!

You see, we must all play our part and be the hands of Jesus extended. The church is filled with imperfect people, but instead of complaining about them, let's step up and be a catalyst of change. Catch a vision, launch a vision, lead a vision, and be a part of lasting change in your city. As Pastor Joel Osteen wrote, "When God puts love and compassion in your heart toward someone, He's offering you an opportunity to make a difference in that person's life. You must learn to follow that love. Don't ignore it. Act on it. Somebody needs what you have."[1] The church is still God's vehicle of hope. It is still the place to find rest and safety in an out-of-control world. There is a community of believers waiting for you to join the vision. Your purpose is not in the four walls of a building, but I do believe that your empowerment can be found there. God still meets His bride at the altar of the church!

Chapter 17

I'VE MADE TOO MANY MISTAKES

P AT, I HAVE done so many bad things; I just never thought God could forgive me. I have been to prison, hurt people who love me, and yet God still loves me! I thought He was mad at me. All of those years I lived in constant guilt." Those were words I heard from my sister just two weeks before she passed away. It broke my heart to know she had lived most of her life believing God couldn't possibly forgive her.

I have met so many people who have the same mind-set. They simply can't conceive that God could love them because they have made so many mistakes in life. Jesus loved hanging out with sinners; on many different occasions in the Bible Jesus ate supper with sinners. And He hung on the cross for *this* sinner. I honestly believe that if Jesus walked on earth today you would find Him in the worst of the worst places. Why? Because He would be wherever people who need Him were, whether that is a penthouse or a crack house.

God doesn't get tired of forgiving. Forgiveness is His love language. He desires that all men walk in freedom (2 Pet. 3:9). And He commands us all to repent (Acts 17:30). What good would it do for us to repent if God weren't willing to forgive? My goal in this chapter is to share with you something so many people have failed to understand—the power of grace!

The great preacher Charles Spurgeon said it well: "There is no other present salvation except that which begins and ends with grace."[1]

God's grace is the most powerful of all the gifts we have been given. What is grace? It is unmerited favor. We didn't earn it; Jesus earned it for us. The Greek word translated "grace" is *charis* (pronounced *khar'-ece*), and it literally means favor, kindness, thanks, and "freely extended to give."[2] You could do nothing of yourself to deserve God's grace or to bestow it on yourself. Because of what Christ did on the cross, you have been given a gift of freedom, and God is just waiting for you to accept it. He has the keys to your prison cell. All you must do is receive them and open the door!

Let me explain it this way. Imagine a terrible crime against humanity has been committed. The crime is sin, and you are the guilty party. Somewhere along the way you didn't use good judgment, and now someone has to pay the price for the sin.

It is all over the local news: "Horrendous Crime Committed!" You realize there is no place to hide and figure you may as well turn yourself in to the proper authorities. Justice finally has caught up with you, and you are in a whole heap of trouble. You are arrested and released on bond, and the court system assigns you a counselor (the Holy Spirit). You have a day in court coming, but in the meantime there are reporters (your conscience) outside your house waiting to get a picture of you or a statement. They are camped out and refuse to leave.

You can't go anywhere without being dogged by your crime (memories). The court of public opinion (peers) has already found you guilty. Finally your day in court (the place of conviction) comes. The judge (God the Father) walks into the courtroom, and everyone expects Him to throw the book at you. After all, you deserve it. You are guilty, and you know it! You ask your counselor to make a way for you to meet with the judge in His chambers.

Permission is granted, and you go to the judge's chambers (the secret place). When you enter the chambers, you fall on your knees and beg the judge for mercy. The judge takes you by the hand and lifts you to your feet. He says, "I know you're guilty, but I forgive you. I will set you free, but someone must take your place."

You and the counselor head back to the courtroom. Your eyes are swollen from weeping, yet you feel acquitted. What you don't realize is that everyone in the courtroom is guilty of the same crime (Rom. 3:10). The difference is that you have asked the judge to forgive you.

The evidence is all there, and He has to convict you. After all, He is a righteous judge. Finally He renders His verdict. The courtroom is silent. He suddenly declares you are guilty, but someone (Jesus) has asked to take your punishment. A commotion breaks out in the courtroom! The judge then declares you are pardoned.

You are guilty and know it, but instead of condemning you, the judge has another plan. He says, "I have decided you can go free because someone else (Jesus) is going to take your punishment." You are in shock. Your record has been wiped clean. You have now gained your freedom. That is called *grace*. The judge looks at you and says, "Now, go and sin no more!"

The courtroom suddenly becomes a place of mass confusion. Protests break out all around you. The people begin to shout, "But he is guilty!" The judge begins to pound His gavel and say, "But I have just delivered this person from the penalty, and it is just as if he never committed the crime! Someone else (Jesus) has chosen to take the place of the prisoner!" That is called *justification*. Jesus has the power to make it just as if we never sinned!

When you accept Christ as your Savior (Rom. 10:9), you are free to go. The apostle Paul said it best in Romans 5:15–17: "But the gift is not like the trespass. For if the many died by the trespass of the one man, how much more did God's grace and the gift that came by the grace of the one man, Jesus Christ, overflow to the many! Again, the gift of God is not like the result of one man's sin: The judgment followed one sin and brought condemnation, but the gift followed many trespasses and brought justification. For if, by the trespass of the one man, death reigned through that one man, how much more will those who receive God's abundant provision of grace and of the gift of righteousness reign in life through the one man, Jesus Christ."

God loves all of us regardless of our history. There is a huge difference between conviction and condemnation. God convicts, and that leads us to repentance, but the devil condemns, and that leads to a life of guilt. You see, the devil is angry, and he is always there to continually condemn you. But you need not worry because the judge has the final say. Look at how the apostle Paul put it in Romans 8:1–3: "Therefore, there is now no condemnation for those who are in Christ Jesus, because through Christ Jesus the law of the Spirit who gives life has set me free from the law of sin and death. For what the law was powerless to do in that it was weakened by the sinful nature, God did by sending his own Son in the likeness of sinful man to be a sin offering. And so he condemned sin in the sinful man." Jesus took our place. Welcome to grace!

GRACE IS FREELY GIVEN

God has called us to be in Him. Jesus said in John 15:5, "I am the vine; you are the branches. If a man remains in me and I in him, he will bear much fruit; apart from me you can do nothing." The only way to remain in God is through grace. And when we remain in Him, we no longer have to be controlled by the things of this world. Romans 6:14 tells us, "For sin shall not be your master, because you are not under law, but under grace."

We live in a day and age when nothing is free. Everything

costs you something. Therefore, for many people it is nearly inconceivable that God would freely forgive them when their mistakes outweigh their victories. But look what Paul tells us in Romans 3:22–24: "This righteousness from God comes through faith in Jesus Christ to all who believe. There is no difference, for all have sinned and fall short of the glory of God, and are justified freely by his grace through the redemption that came by Christ Jesus."

The most valuable thing you will ever receive is God's grace. He gave it to us so we can understand the power of being redeemed. Second Peter 3:17–18 advises us, "Therefore, dear friends, since you already know this, be on your guard so that you may not be carried away by the error of lawless men and fall from your secure position. But grow in the *grace* and knowledge of our Lord and Savior Jesus Christ" (emphasis added).

Grace isn't complicated; it's just hard to believe for all the reasons we've discussed. My prayer is that from this day forward you will realize that your sin has been forgiven and that you will no longer listen to the devil's condemnation. In order to grow in grace, you must remember these seven truths.

1. God gives second chances.

Everybody needs a second chance. Romans 11:30–32 says, "There was a time not so long ago when you were on the outs with God. But then the Jews slammed the door on him and things opened up for you. Now they are on the outs. But with the door held wide open for you, they have a way back in. In one way or another, God makes sure that we all experience what it means to be outside so that he can personally open the door and welcome us back in" (THE MESSAGE). No matter what you've done, God opens the door and says, "Welcome home!"

2. God draws us with His goodness, not His wrath.

God's nature is complete goodness. He isn't angry or walking around with a chip on His shoulder. He loves with an everlasting love. Jeremiah 31:3 tells us that, "The LORD appeared to us in the past, saying: 'I have loved you with an everlasting love; I have drawn you with loving-kindness.'" And the psalmist said of God, "You are good, and what you do is good; teach me your decrees" (Ps. 119:68).

Paul made a profound statement about God's goodness in Romans 2:4. He said, "Do you show contempt for the riches of his kindness, tolerance and patience, not realizing that God's kindness leads you toward repentance?" God's kindness leads us to repentance. We can top that off with this awesome promise given in 1 John 1:5: "This, in essence, is the message we heard from Christ and are passing on to you: God is light, pure light; there's not a trace of darkness in him" (THE MESSAGE). God is absolutely good—there isn't a trace of darkness in Him.

3. God forgives and forgets.

When you accept Christ, He wipes the slate completely clean. It doesn't matter what you have done in your past; God cleans up your record. In Jeremiah 31:34 God gives us this promise, "For I will forgive their wickedness and will remember their sins no more." That verse is saying God has let your sins go. Only you and those affected by your actions remember what you have done in your past. Romans 3:25–26 tells us, "God sacrificed Jesus on the altar of the world to clear that world of sin. Having faith in him sets us in the clear. God decided on this course of action in full view of the public—to set the world in the clear with himself through the sacrifice of Jesus, finally taking care of the sins he had so patiently endured. This is not only clear, but it's now—this is current history! God sets things right. He also makes it possible for us to live in his rightness" (THE MESSAGE). Make no mistake—God has forgiven your sins completely. He's not going to throw your past in your face one day. Because of what Jesus did on the cross, your slate is clean in His eyes.

4. You must walk away from your past.

God wants you to bring everything to Him. He will help you get free of your past and walk in victory. Psalm 55:22 says, "Cast your cares on the LORD and he will sustain you; he will never let the righteous fall." The apostle Paul, a man who once persecuted the church, knew well that we can leave the past behind. He wrote in Philippians 3:13–14: "Brothers, I do not consider myself yet to have taken hold of it. But one thing I do: Forgetting what is behind and straining toward what is ahead, I press on toward the goal to win the prize for which God has called me heavenward in Christ Jesus." God wants us to walk away from our past and press toward Him. He will sustain us as we strain toward the new things He has in store.

If you have messed up in life, if you desire more of God, if you want to experience new life in Christ, let Psalm 119:27–32 become your prayer: "Help me understand these things inside and out so I can ponder your miracle-wonders. My sad life's dilapidated, a falling-down barn; build me up again by your Word. Barricade the road that goes Nowhere; grace me with your clear revelation. I choose the true road to Somewhere, I post your road signs at every curve and corner. I grasp and cling to whatever you tell me; God, don't let me down! I'll run the course you lay out for me if you'll just show me how" (THE MESSAGE). Believe me, He will show you how!

5. You must change your surroundings.

Don't go back to what you used to be. I have heard for years that *your decisions determine your destiny and create your past.* There is a price to pay for sin. It will cost you joy, freedom, power, authority, and the opportunity to spend eternity in heaven. Christ has set us free from sin; He did not free us to see us enslaved again. Galatians 5:1 makes this clear: "Christ has set us free to live a free life. So take your stand! Never again let anyone put a harness of slavery on you" (THE MESSAGE). Always choose to run from what wants to take you back into sin. Even in your weakness, God will help you. Second Corinthians 12:9 says, "He said to me, 'My grace is sufficient for you, for my power is made perfect in weakness.' Therefore I will boast all the more gladly about my weaknesses, so that Christ's power may rest on me." God wants your memories to be full of joy. For that to happen, you must never allow yourself to be enslaved again to sin.

6. God's grace gives you strength for life.

Second Corinthians 9:8 says, "God is able to make all grace abound to you, so that in all things at all times, having all that you need, you will abound every good work." When you walk in the grace of God, life becomes about walking in newness. God wants you to let go and let Him work. He will guide you and direct your path. We just have to obey His Word. Proverbs 3:1–4 says, "Good friend, don't forget all I've taught you; take to heart my commands. They'll help you live a long, long time, a long life lived full and well. Don't lose your grip on Love and Loyalty. Tie them around your neck; carve their initials on your heart. Earn a reputation for living well in God's eyes and the eyes of the people" (THE MESSAGE).

7. If you have received grace, you must extend it to others.

You love Jesus only as much you love your worst enemy. You must extend grace to people and forgive those who have wronged you. Matthew 5:44 says, "Love your enemies and pray for those who persecute you." God wants us to walk in freedom from the pain others may have caused. Jesus said in Matthew 6:14–15, "If you forgive other people when they sin against you, your heavenly Father will also forgive you. But if you do not forgive men their sins, your Father will not forgive your sins." It is time to let go of what has held you back. When you forgive others, you free yourself from the pain they have caused.

The greatest commandments are, "Love the Lord your God with all your heart and with all your soul and with all your strength and with all your mind" and "Love your neighbor as yourself" (Luke 10:27). God has loved you with an everlasting love. Now you must give it away.

You can never make too many mistakes. God's love knows no bounds, and His grace is more than enough to cover anything you may have done wrong. As Romans 5:20 says, "Sin didn't, and doesn't, have a chance in competition with the aggressive forgiveness we call grace. When it's sin versus grace, grace wins hands down. All sin can do is threaten us with death, and that's the end of it. Grace, because God is putting everything together again through the Messiah, invites us into life—a life that goes on and on and on, world without end" (THE MESSAGE).

Chapter 18

GOD ALLOWED ME TO GET SICK

S ON, GOD MUST be mad at me." Those were the words I heard from my precious grandmother after she had been diagnosed with terminal cancer. She simply couldn't understand how she could be sick because she loved God and served Him with all of her heart. I have heard many people ask why God, if He is so loving, allowed them or their loved one to get sick.

It has always been my deepest desire to see people healed of their suffering, and I have been blessed over the years to see many miraculous healings. I have been in services where people have been healed of blindness, cancer, deafness, and other conditions. I know most people don't see those kinds of miracles all the time, but by the end of this chapter I pray at least one thing will be clear to you: sickness does not come from God—He desires to heal our bodies.

When I see a child with twisted limbs as a result of palsy, I want to walk up to that child and lay hands on him and see him set free. But the truth is, at times I question my own faith in God's healing power. I'm going to admit something to you so personal I never thought I'd tell anyone other than my wife, Karen. It concerns our son, Nate.

After years of playing high school and college football, Nate crushed two disks in his back, and that altered the curvature of his spine. He lives in constant pain because of this, and major back surgery is the only way to repair the damage. I have prayed for my son's back over and over, yet he has not been healed. One night Nate called me from college and said, "Dad, please pray; I am really hurting tonight." I prayed for him, but when I got off the phone I asked Karen, "Does God even heal?" We had been waiting so long for Nate's healing.

After I made that statement, I immediately felt God grab my heart. I knew what I had said was wrong. I went straight to my prayer room and began to weep before God. Since that moment God has taken me on a journey to understanding healing. I want to share a bit of what He has taught me about this subject. I believe this chapter will help you understand that sickness is not due to God's anger toward any of us—He's not even angry that you have questions about His willingness to heal. In fact, I am learning that sometimes in our doubt the door of discovery shines much brighter. It is when doubt shifts to expectation that miracles begin to happen.

When you're tempted to doubt that God heals, remember what the psalmist said: "Praise the LORD, O my soul, and forget not all his benefits—*who forgives all your sins and heals all your diseases*, who redeems your life from the pit and crowns you with love and compassion" (Ps. 103:2–4, emphasis added). God not only forgives us, but He will also heal us.

I have wondered at times if there is a formula for healing, but I have found that there is no trick. God wants us to walk in faith, pray faithfully, and stand on His Word.

GOD WANTS TO HEAL

Healing isn't just something that happened in the New Testament. God has been healing since the beginning of time. Look at these promises in Exodus 23:25: "Worship the LORD your God, and his blessing will be on your food and water. *I will take away sickness from among you*" (emphasis added).

Psalm 107:20 says, "He sent forth his word and healed them; he rescued them from the grave." And Jeremiah 30:17 promises, "'I will restore you to health and heal your wounds,' declares the LORD, 'because you are called an outcast, Zion for whom no one cares.'" Healing was promised before the cross, but it was brought into completeness at the cross.

I know God still performs miracles. He loves to heal His children. He doesn't punish the righteous. Sickness is the result of the curse of sin. If we go all the way back to the Garden of Eden in Genesis 1 and 2, there was no sickness. Why? Because there was no sin in the garden until Adam and Eve ate of the forbidden fruit. Sin opened the door to the destruction of not only our souls but also our bodies.

The devil's goal is to take us out. John 10:10 says, "A thief is only there to steal and kill and destroy. I came so they can have real and eternal life, more and better life than they ever dreamed of" (THE MESSAGE). The devil desires to destroy us, but God wants us to have a good life. I find it amazing that so many believers actually believe the opposite of John 10:10. We don't verbalize it and say God came to kill, steal, and destroy, and that the devil came to give us abundant life. That would be absolutely crazy, right? But people say things such as, "God has given me this disease to teach me a lesson." *That is not possible.*

God is not the author of sickness. And let me tell you, if we did to our kids what many people accuse God of doing, we would be put in jail for child abuse. God does not choose to abuse us or make us sick. We live in a fallen world. A loving God wouldn't give us an affliction to teach us something and then not heal us until we learned the lesson. That's completely out of character for Him.

Everything God wanted to teach us about Himself He did through the life of His Son. God revealed His heart through Jesus. In John 14:9 Jesus told Philip, "If you have seen me, then you have seen the Father." And Hebrews 1:3 says Jesus is "the radiance of God's glory and the exact representation of his being, sustaining all things by his powerful word."

Jesus's résumé was all about healing and setting people free. In fact, Jesus performed so many miracles it is impossible to know them all. John 21:25 tells us that "Jesus did many other things as well. If every one of them were written down, I suppose that even the whole world would not have room for the books that would be written." I never saw in Scripture where Jesus told a person who needed healing, "Hey, sir, I would love to heal you right now, but My Father is trying to teach you a lesson and you need more time to learn it. Maybe you should come back later." Acts 10:38 says God anointed Jesus with the Holy Spirit and with power, and He went about doing good and healing all who were oppressed by the devil, for God was with Him.

Evangelist Reinhard Bonnke is one of my spiritual fathers. I believe him to be the greatest evangelist of our lifetime. Pastor Bonnke has preached all over the world, and millions have been saved and healed as a result of his ministry. He has literally seen people raised from the dead. He truly is a man of powerful faith. One day while we were meeting, I asked him how he got ready for a service and how he prepared to see miracles. I've never forgotten what he said. He told me, "Every time I show up to a crusade with hundreds of thousands of people, I understand that God always shows up at His best. Therefore when I show up, I should be at my very best. God is always ready to do the supernatural, so I must be ready. I never complain, and I always expect the supernatural. I live in a state of readiness!"[1] I love that! God always shows up at His best! That challenged me more than you could ever know. Pastor Bonnke went on to say we must expect God to show up in His fullness. He said, "We always act like God only shows up in percentages in our services. We say things like, 'I didn't feel God today in our service.' This is impossible. He is always there. He doesn't show up in percentages. He is a whole God. We always invite Him in, and this is like inviting someone into a place when He is already there. It is foolishness! God is already there! The question isn't whether God is there, but the question is, are we?"[2]

That is what I call supernatural faith! It's difficult to imagine how far the church has fallen in two thousand years. What has happened to the miraculous? What has happened to our authority? If you look back over church history, you see great leaders such as John Alexander Dowie, Aimee Semple McPherson, and Smith Wigglesworth, who all walked in the power of healing. These were people who had incredible healing ministries, and one thing they had in common—one common denominator—was that they believed all sickness is from the devil.

The New Testament was written originally in Greek, and *sōtēria*, one of the words translated "salvation," literally means:

1. Deliverance, preservation, safety, salvation

2. Preservation (of physical life), safety[3]

Look at Psalm 103:2–3 again. It says, "Praise the LORD, O my soul, and forget not all his benefits—who forgives all your sins and heals all your diseases." Sickness and disease are mentioned in the same breath as sin. In other words, if God can forgive our sins, then He can heal our diseases. It's a whole new way of thinking about healing and miracles.

Someone may say, "My great-aunt developed cancer and died, but it brought our family together, so God must have wanted her to get sick." That type of thinking is wrong. We know that Romans 8:28 says God works everything for His good, but that doesn't mean He causes sickness. It's that kind of thinking that has given the devil so much room to steal and destroy!

I am always amazed at the miracles that take place in third world countries—the blind see, the lame walk, the deaf hear.

What is keeping the American church from experiencing these kinds of supernatural events? I believe one reason is that leaders who lack inner healing have corrupted the gift! You cannot give away what you do not possess. Leaders too must break free of doubt and fear. I've found that there are three things that attack leaders when they pray for people:

- Self-doubt about the purity of their lives
- Self-doubt about their faith
- Self-doubt about whether God can trust them with the miracle

Jesus came to set us free from those doubts. There is a battle raging against what we believe. The war is constant. But we must understand that the cross is more than a get-out-of-hell-free card. It has given us access to total forgiveness and supernatural power! The devil is constantly trying to get us to focus on our inadequacies, but God is calling His church to experience complete freedom from all of those fears—so the world can experience His healing power!

JESUS WON THE VICTORY OVER SICKNESS ON THE CROSS

When it comes to God's power and His desire to heal, there is a powerful truth that you must understand: Jesus won the victory over sickness on the cross! What began as a selfish act under a tree ended with a selfless act on a tree! Adam and Eve's actions in the garden made us slaves to sin, but Jesus bought our freedom. Galatians 3:13 says, "Christ redeemed us from the curse of the law by becoming a curse for us, for it is written: 'Cursed is everyone who is hung on a tree.'" (See also Deuteronomy 21:23.)

The apostle Paul wrote in Romans 8:3–5 that "what the law was powerless to do...God did by sending his own

Son in the likeness of sinful man to be a sin offering. And so he condemned sin in sinful man, in order that the righteous requirement of the law might be fully met in us, who do not live according to the sinful nature but according to the Spirit. Those who live according to the sinful nature have their minds set on what that nature desires; but those who live in accordance with the Spirit have their minds set on what the Spirit desires." We broke the law, and Jesus was condemned to death for it. The problem is we still live in bondage to what He destroyed!

At the cross Jesus won the victory for us. Through His death Jesus:

- Gave us freedom over sin

- Gave us freedom over death, hell, and the grave

- Gave us freedom over our thoughts (represented by the crown of thorns)

- Gave us freedom over what we do with our hands (symbolized by the nails put in His hands)

- Grafted us into His family (signified by the piercing Jesus received in His side)

But in order to understand how Jesus secured our healing at Calvary, we must take a look at the backside of the cross. So many times we look at the front of the cross for our salvation and forget that the backside of the cross brought our healing! The cross was a complete work. Some twenty-seven hundred years before Christ went to the cross, the prophet Isaiah foresaw the most horrible and most powerful day to ever befall humanity. On that day the sin that had entered the world in the Garden of Eden would be abolished. On that day mankind's separation from God would be annulled. And on that day healing would be ripped into a Savior! The prophet Isaiah declared:

> The servant grew up before God—a scrawny seedling, a scrubby plant in a parched field. There was nothing attractive about him, nothing to cause us to take a second look. He was looked down on and passed over, a man who suffered, who knew pain firsthand. One look at him and people turned away. We looked down on him, thought he was scum. But the fact is, it was our pains he carried— our disfigurements, all the things wrong with us. We thought he brought it on himself, that God was punishing him for his own failures. But it was our sins that did that to him, that ripped and tore and crushed him—our sins! He took the punishment, and that made us whole. Through his bruises we get healed. We're all like sheep who've wandered off and gotten lost. We've all done our own thing, gone our own way. And God has piled all our sins, everything we've done wrong, on him, on him.
> —ISAIAH 53:2–6, THE MESSAGE

This prophecy would be fulfilled on the day Christ was crucified for you and me. The Roman soldiers took Jesus and tied Him to a whipping post. They beat Him with a cat-o'-nine-tails that had shards of metal and glass in it. That means every time He was struck with this whip, it would attach itself to His flesh. Then the Roman soldiers would yank it out to strike Jesus all over again, each time ripping massive amounts of flesh from His back.

The scourging would continue until Jesus had been hit thirty-nine times; the beating was so bad it left our Savior virtually unrecognizable. I used to read the passage in Isaiah 53 and not understand why it said, "By His stripes we are healed" (v. 5, NKJV), right in the middle of all the reasons we are forgiven of our sins. Then I began to realize something.

Sin is to the soul what sickness is to the body. First Peter 2:24 says, "He himself bore our sins in his body on the tree, so that we might die to sins and live for righteousness; by his wounds you have been healed." Please understand this: whatever your sickness or affliction may be, Jesus paid for your healing on the cross along with your deliverance and salvation.

There is no formula that will bring miraculous healing, but I want to share three truths we must remember if we want to see the supernatural power of God manifest in our lives.

1. We must walk in supernatural faith!

Romans 10:17 says, "Faith comes from hearing the message, and the message is heard through the word of Christ." First Peter 2:24 tells us, just as Isaiah 53 did, that by Jesus's stripes we have been healed. Our responsibility now is to believe it. That is what it means to walk by faith. Hebrews 11:1 says faith is "being sure of what we hope for and certain of what we do not see." Without this faith, it is impossible to please God or have confidence in His ability to heal. We cannot spend our energy doubting God's Word. We must believe God and walk in supernatural faith.

2. We must speak life!

Jesus said in Matthew 18:19, "If two of you on earth agree about anything you ask for, it will be done for you by my Father in heaven." We must learn that there is power in our tongues. Proverbs 18:21 says, "Death and life are in the power of the tongue: and they that love it shall eat the fruit thereof" (KJV). That's so important I want to say it again: *life and death are in the power of your tongue.* Many times we misquote that verse and say the power of life and death are in the tongue, but life and death have no power in themselves. The power lies in your tongue; it has the ability to produce or create death or life. Hebrews 11:3 says, "By faith we understand that the worlds were framed by the word of God" (NKJV). You also have the power to frame your world! Proverbs 6:2 says, "You are snared by the words of your mouth" (NKJV). It is so critical that we guard how we use our tongue. Words have life! I challenge you to declare life over every situation that you find yourself in.

3. We cannot forsake the laying on of hands!

An important instruction about healing is found in James 5:14–16: "Is anyone among you sick? Let him call for the elders of the church, and let them pray over him, anointing him with oil in the name of the Lord. And the prayer of faith will save the sick, and the Lord will raise him up" (NKJV). Jesus often laid hands on people before healing them (Mark 6:5; Luke 4:40; 13:13). If you are sick, ask someone to lay hands on you and pray for your healing! Mark 16:17–18 tells us certain signs shall follow those who believe; one of them is that "they shall lay hands on the sick, and they shall recover" (KJV). Don't underestimate what God can do through the laying on of hands.

SICKNESS AND PAIN WON'T LAST FOREVER

Because we live in a fallen world, sickness and disease are a part of our lives. But we do not experience sickness and pain because God is mad at us! Sickness is not from God; it is from the enemy! God made a way for our healing, and He gave us His Spirit to help us hold on through whatever we're facing. The apostle Paul, who lived with a thorn in his flesh (2 Cor. 12:7), spoke of his desire to be in heaven, but he knew he had work on earth to do. In Philippians 1:23–26 he says, "I am torn between the two: I desire to depart and be with Christ, which is better by far; but it is more necessary for you that I remain in the body. Convinced of this, I know that I will remain, and I will continue with all of you for your progress and joy in the faith, so that through my being with you again your joy in Christ Jesus will overflow on account of me."

The Lord will call you home when He is ready for you; until then He has work for you to do here on earth. There will come a time when sickness, pain, and death will pass away. In the meantime you must realize God has a plan. Use what you have been through to help others! Our sorrow can be redemptive if we understand that God will use it to enrich and bring healing to others. Today, no matter what you are facing, hold on! The situation is only temporary. Remember this promise you have been given in Luke 21:28, "When these things begin to take place, stand up and lift up your heads, because *your redemption is drawing near*" (emphasis added).

CHAPTER 19

THE DEVIL IS A LIAR!

OST PEOPLE DO not realize that we are in a constant state of mortal combat. The devil is the enemy of all of creation. He has but one goal, and it is to kill, steal, and destroy (John 10:10). There was a time when he was the chief angel and worship leader of heaven. He had power and authority. The Book of Ezekiel tells us Satan was once anointed as a guardian cherub, and that he was "on the holy mount of God" and "walked among the fiery stones" (Ezek. 28:14).

But the devil was hurled down from heaven when he and one-third of the angels revolted against God and His authority (Luke 10:18). Isaiah 14:12–14 describes the devil's rebellion and demise this way: "How you have fallen from heaven, O morning star, son of the dawn! You have been cast down to the earth, you who once laid low the nations! You said in your heart, 'I will ascend to heaven; I will raise my throne above the stars of God; I will sit enthroned on the mount of assembly, on the utmost heights of the sacred mountain.'"

I think it is safe to assume the devil has an ax to grind. And his plan includes destroying you and me! One of the biggest and most overlooked reasons many people believe God is mad at them is simply because the devil is a liar. He loves to

WHY IS GOD SO MAD AT ME?

manipulate people's minds. He's been doing it since Genesis 3 when he deceived Adam and Eve and provoked the fall of mankind!

God vowed at that moment to punish Satan (Gen. 3:15), and Jesus fulfilled that prophecy on the cross! He won the victory over the devil on the cross, but as long as we are on this earth, we will have to deal with the devil's attacks. Why? The devil is the god of this age. He has blinded people to the truth. Second Corinthians 4:4 says, "The god of this age has blinded the minds of unbelievers, so that they cannot see the light of the gospel of the glory of Christ, who is the image of God." How has he blinded people? He gets them to believe his lies are the truth!

The devil would love for you to believe you are a failure, useless, ugly, dumb, and worthless, and that you will never get free. This is how he has convinced a generation to harm themselves and make destructive choices. The apostle Paul asked the Galatians what got them off the good path they were on as followers of Jesus. "You were running a good race," he said. "Who cut in on you and kept you from obeying the truth? That kind of persuasion does not come from the one who calls you" (Gal. 5:7–8). The Galatian church had fallen for the devil's persuasive lies, and now they were no longer walking in the truth.

Satan will do everything he can to deceive you into believing God is not real or that He couldn't care less about you! The devil steals, kills, and destroys. That is what he does. He will steal your life, kill your dreams, and destroy your future. He is a liar. He will tell you that even if God is real, you have made too many mistakes to receive His love. He will lie and lie and lie until you're finally convinced that God is mad at you!

THE TRUTH IS NOT IN HIM!

Jesus made sure to always make a show of Satan. In John 8, while confronting some religious guys, Jesus laid out the devil's résumé, saying, "He was a murderer from the beginning, not holding to the truth, for there is no truth in him. When he lies, he speaks his native language, for he is a liar and the father of lies" (vv. 43–44).

The truth is not in him. He tried to deceive Jesus after He had been in the wilderness fasting forty days and forty nights (Matt. 4), but Jesus withstood his attack by declaring the truth of God's Word! The challenge for us is that the enemy isn't always as easy to recognize as he was when he came to tempt Jesus. He loves to disguise himself. He will attack us with negative thoughts and fears. He will cause us to question God's Word and plant doubt in our minds. If he came to us as he really is, we would be repulsed, so he uses trickery and deception. Second Corinthians 11:14 tells us, "Satan himself masquerades as an angel of light."

The devil has been lying to you since you were born! I've known people who thought they were ugly or stupid or unlovable for as long as they can remember. That's no accident. The devil has been lying to them, trying to divert them from their destiny before they even knew what was happening. The devil doesn't take vacations. He is always on the attack! He desires to distract and tempt you so you'll separate from God, and he'll use any tool he can find.

All temptation to sin is based on a lie from the devil, a lie promising something it cannot deliver. The devil hopes you never understand that *nothing* can separate you from the love of God (Rom. 8:39)! He will do everything he can to convince you that he knows best. That is why we must always keep our thoughts on God.

The apostle Paul wrote in Romans 12 that you must transform your mind by renewing it. But he said you also have to crucify your flesh! We must discipline our thinking and choose not to believe anything that doesn't line up with what God says about who we are and who we are called to be. Colossians 3:2 says, "Set your minds on things above, not on earthly things."

Galatians 5:24 adds that "those who belong to Christ Jesus have crucified the sinful nature with its passions and desires." That literally means that you do what Christ did for you! You lay down your life to fulfill God's plan, ignoring the desires the devil sends your way!

STAND YOUR GROUND

The Bible tells us that the spiritual battle we are in is unbelievably intense, and we can't fight with normal weapons! Ephesians 6:12 tell us "our struggle is not against flesh and blood, but against the rulers, against the authorities, against the powers of this dark world and against the spiritual forces of evil in the heavenly realms."

Revelation 12:10 calls Satan "the accuser of our brethren" (NKJV). The word "accuser" in the Greek language is *kategoros*; it can also mean "prosecutor."[1] "The word "devil" in the Greek is *diablos,* which means false accuser or slanderer.[2] The devil will always accuse you of being what *he* is! Any accusation he brings against you is a definition of what he represents. Ignore him!

I want you to understand that the devil is out to destroy you. He has convinced many in this generation that God is mad at them, but God has called us to stand in victory against our enemy. You have the power to stand your ground and defeat the enemy. Ephesians 6 explains how we can win this battle.

> Therefore put on the full armor of God, so that when the day of evil comes, you may be able to stand your ground, and after you have done everything, to stand. Stand firm then, with the belt of truth buckled

around your waist, with the breastplate of righteousness in place, and with your feet fitted with the readiness that comes from the gospel of peace. In addition
to all this, take up the shield of faith, with which you
can extinguish all the flaming arrows of the evil one.
Take the helmet of salvation and the sword of the
Spirit, which is the word of God. And pray in the
Spirit on all occasions with all kinds of prayers and
requests. With this in mind, be alert and always keep
on praying for all the saints.

—EPHESIANS 6:13-18

God says, "Pray in the Spirit on all occasions!" That is a
direct order. That is how you fight! Know who you are in
Christ and declare it in the face of the devil's lies. That's how
you will overcome the enemy.

We all know the devil does not win the war. God wins,
and if you are on God's team, then you win too! God has
given you the power to walk upon the devil! Before he fell
and became known as Satan, Lucifer was described in Ezekiel
28:13 as being adorned with twelve precious stones. As he
would stand before God, the light of God would hit his body
and he would reflect God's light off the jewels that adorned
him. It had to have been a glorious sight. It's obvious that
God created Lucifer to reflect the beauty of the Lord. But
then he was forced from heaven in disgrace.

What I am about to share with you will show you just how
amazing our God is and how well He takes care of His children. The Bible says in Revelation 21:19–20 that the foun-
dations of the city of God in heaven are covered in twelve
precious jewels. They are the same jewels that once covered
the devil. This is truly incredible! God loves us so much that
He allows us to walk on the very jewels that adorned the devil!

A friend of mine named Glyn Barrett, who is a great leader
and pastor in the United Kingdom, wrote a powerful book for

students called *If I Was the Devil*. In the book he addresses
several truths the devil doesn't want you to know. Glyn writes
that the devil would make you a victim instead of a victor; he
would distract you and help you find excuses. He'd get you to
compare yourself to others and make you think you have lots
of time to get right with God. That's just how the devil works.[3]

Those are the very tools he has used to delude this generation. The devil has more tricks in his arsenal, and Glyn shares
eight of them in his great book. I encourage you to read it to
guard yourself against the enemy's schemes. The devil is a liar,
and he operates through deception. Let him know enough is
enough. Draw a line in the sand and say, "I will no longer be
your puppet! God has chosen me to walk in freedom!"

The devil really is under your feet. So the next time Satan
brings thoughts of destruction, just remind him that his time
is running out. John tells us how the devil's story ends in
Revelation 12:10–12: "Then I heard a loud voice in heaven say:
'Now have come the salvation and the power and the kingdom
of our God, and the authority of his Christ. *For the accuser
of our brothers, who accuses them before our God day and night,
has been hurled down. They overcame him by the blood of the
Lamb and by the word of their testimony*'" (emphasis added).

God isn't mad at you, but the devil sure is ticked at all
of us! Your testimony of how God gave you freedom is the
devil's demise! Open your mouth and declare God's awesome
power! God will protect you. According to Isaiah 54:17, "'No
weapon forged against you will prevail, and you will refute
every tongue that accuses you. This is the heritage of the servants of the LORD, and this is their vindication from me,'
declares the LORD."

PART 4

AWAKEN TO NEW LIFE

Chapter 20

DOES GOD GET MAD?

THROUGHOUT THIS BOOK I've tried to get you to see that God is not mad at you, but that doesn't mean God does not get mad. There are many people today who would love for you to believe that God doesn't experience the same emotions as human beings do because He is an existential God. But that simply is not true. How could He be moved by our infirmities if He didn't also experience what we experience? God has suffered with us. Isaiah 63:9 says, "In all their distress he too was distressed, and the angel of his presence saved them. In his love and mercy he redeemed them; he lifted them up and carried them all the days of old." That verse proves that God experiences the same emotions as we do.

We know that God grew angry with nations that stood against Him or His people. King David cried out, "Arise, O LORD, in your anger; rise up against the rage of my enemies. Awake, my God; decree justice" (Ps. 7:6). God not only gets angry, but He also inflicts justice. God even hates certain things! Proverbs 6:16–19 says, "There are six things the LORD hates, seven that are detestable to him: haughty eyes, a lying tongue, hands that shed innocent blood, a heart that devises wicked schemes, feet that are quick to rush into evil, a false witness who pours out lies and a man who stirs up dissension among brothers."

God hates injustice, and He hates attitudes and actions that destroy mankind. But He doesn't hate you and me. He loves us but hates actions that lead us away from Him. He is a jealous God (Exod. 20:4–6)!

Jesus was both human and divine. He came wrapped in flesh so that He could experience life as we do. This is truly what makes the cross so sweet. Jesus bore God's wrath on our behalf while on the cross. He became human like you and me so He could take the punishment for our sins (2 Cor. 5:21).

Jesus suffered in every way humans suffer and experienced the same highs and lows we do. In the Garden of Gethsemane the weight of our sin was so heavy and the turmoil over being separated from the Father so agonizing that He begged His Father to let Him escape the pain. He even sweat drops of blood (Luke 22:44). All of this shows us that Jesus was very human. Yet He never allowed His suffering to keep Him from His goal of seeing humanity saved. In Luke 22:42 He prayed, "Not my will, but yours be done."

We also know Jesus got angry while He walked the earth. When you read the Gospels, you can tell that on some days He'd had just about enough of the disciples' antics. He would say things such as, "Do you not even realize who I am?" or, "You have such little faith," or, "Cursed is the tree that doesn't produce fruit!"

His greatest show of emotional anger was when He walked into the temple and found that the priests were defrauding people by inflating the prices of sacrificial animals. That really set Him off. He told the religious leaders they were making God's house "a den of robbers" (Matt. 21:13). The Bible says He made a whip and ran the people out of the temple. I guess Jesus understood the deodorant slogan "We must protect this house!"

Jesus got aggravated when the disciples tried to keep the

children from drawing close to Him, and He showed His deep anger for anyone who would harm a child in any way. In Matthew 18:6 Jesus said, "If anyone causes one of these little ones who believe in me to sin, it would be better for him to have a large millstone hung around his neck and to be drowned in the depths of the sea."

Yet every time Jesus got angry in Scripture, He wasn't mad at an individual but at the actions of individuals. He even tried to give His nemeses the Pharisees opportunities to change. If Jesus had wanted to, He could have wiped out all of humanity with a wave of His hand, but He had compassion on us. Have you ever thought about this? Jesus created the soldiers who crucified Him, He created the wood that He died upon, and He even created the elements to make the nails that pierced Him. Yet He still died for you and me.

Chapter 21

FIVE WAYS GOD PROVES
HE'S NOT MAD AT YOU

IN EPHESIANS 3 the apostle Paul prayed that God's people would "grasp how wide and long and high and deep is the love of Christ, and to know this love that surpasses knowledge—that [they] may be filled to the measure of all the fullness of God" (vv. 18–19). Those verses are a powerful picture of the depths of God's love. God doesn't desire to reject you or shame and punish you; God simply desires to hold you!

This entire book was written to prove one major point: God is not mad at you! I wanted to examine the most common reasons people think God is angry with them, but the truth is, I could have simply shared two powerful stories in the Bible because they beautifully illustrate the message of this book. The first story is of the woman who was caught in adultery. The law demanded that she should be stoned, but Jesus had mercy upon her and in doing so also exposed the hypocrisy of the religious leaders.

> The religion scholars and Pharisees led in a woman who had been caught in an act of adultery. They stood her in plain sight of everyone and said, "Teacher, this woman was caught red-handed in the act of adultery. Moses, in the Law, gives orders to stone such persons.

What do you say?" They were trying to trap him into saying something incriminating so they could bring charges against him. Jesus bent down and wrote with his finger in the dirt. They kept at him, badgering him. He straightened up and said, "The sinless one among you, go first: Throw the stone." Bending down again, he wrote some more in the dirt. Hearing that, they walked away, one after another, beginning with the oldest. The woman was left alone. Jesus stood up and spoke to her. "Woman, where are they? Does no one condemn you?" "No one, Master." "Neither do I," said Jesus. "Go on your way. From now on, don't sin."

—JOHN 8:3-11, THE MESSAGE

Don't you just love that? What Jesus said completely set her free. She was the worst of the worst. In fact, what she did will still get a woman killed in some countries. Yet out of His mercy, grace, and love Jesus forgave her. Many people who think God is mad at them have done nothing wrong; they have simply believed the devil's lies. This woman actually had sinned, yet God wasn't mad at her. He defended her against her accusers and gave her another chance. That is the same kind of love the Father has for you and me.

The second story is of the lost son. Here was a young man who messed up badly. Jesus told this story to show that He will welcome us back regardless of our mistakes. The Bible tells us this young man had run off to a distant land. During that time he had blown his money and ruined his life. He broke the law by squandering his inheritance. This was shameful according to Jewish custom. Now he was living on a farm working with pigs. Yet my favorite part is the way the dad (God) responded. He watched and waited for his son every day, and when he finally saw him off in the distance, he couldn't wait to embrace him!

He was so hungry he would have eaten the corn-
cobs in the pig slop, but no one would give him any.
That brought him to his senses. He said, "All those
farmhands working for my father sit down to three
meals a day, and here I am starving to death. I'm
going back to my father. I'll say to him, Father, I've
sinned against God, I've sinned before you; I don't
deserve to be called your son. Take me on as a hired
hand." He got right up and went home to his father.
When he was still a long way off, his father saw him.
His heart pounding, he ran out, embraced him, and
kissed him. The son started his speech: "Father, I've
sinned against God, I've sinned before you; I don't
deserve to be called your son ever again." But the
father wasn't listening. He was calling to the servants,
"Quick. Bring a clean set of clothes and dress him.
Put the family ring on his finger and sandals on his
feet. Then get a grain-fed heifer and roast it. We're
going to feast! We're going to have a wonderful time!
My son is here—given up for dead and now alive!
Given up for lost and now found!" And they began to
have a wonderful time.

—Luke 15:16–24, The Message

Can you imagine that? Every day that father stood at the
edge of the hill waiting for his son. Then, finally, after months
or even years, there he was. The boy was broken, dirty, and
worthless to the world. Yet when the father saw him, he saw
his precious child. He never gave up hope for his son to return
home, and now there he was! That story paints a picture of
a Father who doesn't give up on us, who doesn't cast us off
when we miss it. It paints a picture of a loving Father who
can't wait for the day when His child finally decides to come
home to Him and receive His love!

IT DOESN'T MATTER WHAT YOU'VE DONE

I shared those two stories because God wants you to know that no matter what you have done, He will never leave you or forsake you. That is God's heart for you and me. He is waiting. He is watching. He will accept you back in. He isn't mad at you. Nope! He is mad *about* you! You are the apple of His eye. He created you so He could have a relationship with you. He is a good Dad. I want to spend the rest of this chapter sharing five ways God proves He isn't mad at you.

1. God never stops loving you.

No matter where you are from, where you have been, or the mistakes you have made, God loves you. There is nothing that can get in the way of that. Romans 8:38–39 says, "For I am convinced that neither death nor life, neither angels nor demons, neither the present nor the future, nor any powers, neither height nor depth, nor anything else in all creation, will be able to separate us from the love of God that is in Christ Jesus our Lord." Nothing means *nothing*. In 1 John 4:8 the apostle John makes a very profound statement: "Whoever does not love does not know God, because *God is love*" (emphasis added). In fact, the chapter goes on to say, "We love because He first loved us" (v. 19). God *is* love, and His love for us has no limit.

2. God created you for a purpose.

When Paul was confronting the philosophers of the day at a place called Mars Hill, he painted a vivid picture for them of who God is. He said: "The God who made the world and everything in it, this Master of sky and land, doesn't live in custom-made shrines or need the human race to run errands for him, as if he couldn't take care of himself. He makes the creatures; the creatures don't make him. Starting from scratch, he made the entire human race and made the earth hospitable, with plenty of time and space for living so we could seek after

God, and not just grope around in the dark but actually find him. He doesn't play hide-and-seek with us. He's not remote; he's near. We live and move in him, can't get away from him! One of your poets said it well: 'We're the God-created.' Well, if we are the God-created, it doesn't make a lot of sense to think we could hire a sculptor to chisel a god out of stone for us, does it?" (Acts 17:24–29, THE MESSAGE).

You are "the God-created," and He made you with a destiny and purpose in mind. He didn't create you to sit and do nothing. He chose you to walk in power, freedom, and victory. He has a plan for you and your family. God reveals His purpose through your gifts and talents. What brings you joy? That may be the very thing God has called you to do. I challenge you to use your abilities to bring God glory. That doesn't mean you have to preach, sing, or do drama; it just means you make yourself available to be used by Him. God doesn't use the qualified; He qualifies the called.

3. God wants to give you an abundant life!

The devil would love to destroy you, but God wants you to have an abundant life that is filled with His power and provision! John 10:10 says, "The thief comes only to steal and kill and destroy; I have come that they may have life, and have it to the full." There is not a single need you have that God doesn't want to fulfill. Psalm 145:15–16 confirms this when it says, "The eyes of all look to you, and you give them their food at the proper time. You open your hand and satisfy the desires of every living thing."

God will do more for you than you can imagine. Ephesians 3:20 says God "is able to do immeasurably more than all we ask or imagine, according to his power that is at work within us." In Philippians 4:19 God promises that He will take care of every one of your needs "according to his glorious riches in Christ Jesus." As my dear friend Dave Martin always says, "The rest of your life is the best of your life!" Believe that God will provide all that you need and get ready to live at another level.

4. God gave His Son as a sacrifice to cover all your sins!

God loved you and me so much that He sent His Son to die for us (John 3:16). We had no way to God, but Jesus made it possible, and this pleased God. Ephesians 1:4–5 says, "Because of his love God had already decided that through Jesus Christ he would make us his children—this was his pleasure and purpose" (GNT). I referred to this scripture before, but I want you to see once again how the prophet Isaiah so beautifully described what Jesus endured for you and me.

> The servant grew up before God—a scrawny seedling, a scrubby plant in a parched field. There was nothing attractive about him, nothing to cause us to take a second look. He was looked down on and passed over, a man who suffered, who knew pain firsthand. One look at him and people turned away. We looked down on him, thought he was scum. But the fact is, it was our pains he carried—our disfigurements, all the things wrong with us. We thought he brought it on himself, that God was punishing him for his own failures. But it was our sins that did that to him, that ripped and tore and crushed him—our sins! He took the punishment, and that made us whole. Through his bruises we get healed. We're all like sheep who've wandered off and gotten lost. We've all done our own thing, gone our own way. And God has piled all our sins, everything we've done wrong, on him, on him!
> —ISAIAH 53:2–3, THE MESSAGE

Jesus took our pain and sorrow, and He became the sacrifice that brings us freedom. I love the way Romans 8:3–4 explains what Jesus did. It says, "God went for the jugular when he sent his own Son. He didn't deal with the problem as something remote and unimportant. In his Son, Jesus, he personally took on the human condition, entered the disordered mess of struggling humanity in order to set it right once and for all. The law code, weakened as it always was by fractured human nature, could never have done that" (THE MESSAGE). The guy in me loves the first part of that verse—"God went for the jugular"! That phrase perfectly describes the bold and intense moment when Jesus stepped into our humanity and broke the law to rescue you and me! And He did that because He loved us.

5. God has prepared a place in heaven for you.

This earth is not our home! God prepared something else for us. He prepared a place where we will be able to spend eternity with our loving and faithful Father! Jesus is getting my house ready for me right now. Look at this promise in John 14:1–4: "Don't let this throw you. You trust God, don't you? Trust me. There is plenty of room for you in my Father's home. If that weren't so, would I have told you that I'm on my way to get a room ready for you? And if I'm on my way to get your room ready, I'll come back and get you so you can live where I live. And you already know the road I'm taking" (THE MESSAGE). If you have ever doubted the existence of heaven, just read the entire book of Revelation.

There will come a time when God will call us home to be with Him. First Thessalonians 4:15–17 says, "The Master himself will give the command. Archangel thunder! God's trumpet blast! He'll come down from heaven and the dead in Christ will rise—they'll go first. Then the rest of us who are still alive at the time will be caught up with them into the clouds to meet the Master. Oh, we'll be walking on air! And then there will be one huge family reunion with the Master. So reassure one another with these words" (THE MESSAGE).

This is our promise! That is why the apostle Paul said, "Hey, make sure you tell each other about this. Encourage each other! We are biding our time for a greater place that awaits us."

The writer of Hebrews wrote of those who had stood the test of faith. None of them received all that God had promised them, yet they died still believing. The Bible says they were able to have this kind of faith because they knew they were transients in this world. "People who live this way make it plain that they are looking for their true home. If they were homesick for the old country, they could have gone back any time they wanted. But they were after a far better country than that—heaven country. You can see why God is so proud of them, and has a City waiting for them" (Heb. 11:13–16, THE MESSAGE).

God isn't mad at you. He wants to spend eternity with you. Would you want to live forever with someone you were mad at? God doesn't either. He wants you to be with Him because He delights in you.

Chapter 22

IT'S TIME TO WAKE UP!

WHEN WE UNDERSTAND that God is not mad at us, the next step is to realize that He has called us to awaken to Him. I believe this chapter is going to stir you to move to the next level! Get ready for God to transform you.

Psalm 57:8 says, "Awake, my soul! Awake, harp and lyre! I will awaken the dawn." There is nothing more powerful than a person who gets liberated from guilt and suddenly realizes there is life outside of darkness! Throughout this book I have shared that God has a plan, vision, and purpose for your life. Through good and bad times He stands with you. Now I want you to understand that He wants you to wake up to what He wants to do in your life.

Sometimes God has to shake us out of our slumber. Now is the time to get up! As the apostle Paul said in Romans 13:11–14: "Make sure that you don't get so absorbed and exhausted in taking care of all your day-by-day obligations that you lose track of the time and doze off, oblivious to God. The night is about over, dawn is about to break. Be up and awake to what God is doing! God is putting the finishing touches on the salvation work he began when we first believed. We can't afford to waste a minute, must not squander these precious daylight hours in frivolity and indulgence, in sleeping around and dissipation, in bickering and grabbing everything in sight. Get out of bed and get dressed! Don't loiter and linger, waiting until the very last minute. Dress yourselves in Christ, and be up and about!" (THE MESSAGE).

This passage is a clarion call. No more slumber! This is your moment!

There is an obnoxious board game my family likes to play called "Don't Wake Daddy." The game board is laced with obstacles each player must pass through, and in the middle of the board is a plastic bed with a man lying on it. At the foot of the bed is a button you push if you land on a certain space. The little mechanical bed is designed to pop the man up out of the bed if you push it too many times. The goal of the game is to get through the various obstacles without waking the daddy in the bed. Waking the daddy will not only startle everyone playing, but the person who wakes him up will have to start all over in the game.

This is a fun game that has provided hours of fun in our home, but it brings a sobering thought to mind. Our homes need an awakening. In a time when moms and dads are overwhelmed with finances, when teens hide in their bedrooms and children spend endless hours on the computer, we must awaken to life. I have learned that if the devil can't make you sin, then he will just make you busy! I say, "Wake up, Daddy! Wake up, Mom! Wake up the kids. God has a plan for your entire home."

The world we live in is in turmoil. Religions are fighting religions, a nuclear Iran poses a constant threat, and morality is being dismissed as an obstacle to self-actualization. Hedonism runs rampant from Hollywood to the strip club down the street. Every day there are reports of another child disappearing or an injustice taking place in some alleyway. We have to continually change the TV channel to protect the minds and souls of our children. Our only hope is God.

The day of living as quiet, tired, weary, angry people is over.

God has called us to be different. We serve a living God! We do not worship a concept, a dead idol, or just some religious theory. Have you ever felt the way the psalmist did in Psalm 84:2—"My soul yearns, even faints, for the courts of the LORD; my heart and my flesh cry out for the living God"? I have felt that way!

It seems the enemy is wearing us out. We are like the soldiers in Gideon's army who were "faint, yet pursuing" (Judg. 8:4, KJV). Daniel 7:25 tells us the enemy will do everything he can to wear out the saints, and I am seeing weariness in the body of Christ. The problem is that when we allow darkness to invade our lives, the memories of the "God moments" we've had, those times when we have seen God deliver us and bring the victory, fade into the shadows. Those victories seem to disappear into the abyss of pain. That is why we must remind ourselves of the great things God has done. We must awaken to the power of God!

We must be His light. We are to invade the darkness. Matthew 5:14–16 says, "You are the light of the world. A city on a hill cannot be hidden. Neither do people light a lamp and put it under a bowl. Instead they put it on its stand, and it gives light to everyone in the house. In the same way, let your light shine before men, that they may see your good deeds and praise your Father in heaven." The Bible says that as my light shines, it will cause others to praise God. Psalm 89:15 tells us that blessed are those who have learned to acclaim the Lord, who walk in the light of His presence.

GOD IS STILL SEPARATING LIGHT FROM DARKNESS

There is a separation coming. Those are strong words, I know, but they are true. If we are called to be a light for God, then we must realize that God will separate light from darkness just as He did when He created the heavens and the earth (Gen. 1:4).

Jesus shared a powerful parable concerning this coming separation in Matthew 13 when he told the story of a man who sowed good seed in his field. "But while everyone was sleeping, his enemy came and sowed weeds among the wheat, and went away. When the wheat sprouted and formed heads, then the weeds also appeared" (vv. 25–26). The enemy loves to sow seeds of death in our fields while we are asleep. He desires to destroy the crop that God has planted. Let's keep reading the story.

"So the servants of the owner came and said to him, 'Sir, did you not sow good seed in your field? How then does it have tares?' He said to them, 'An enemy has done this.' The servants said to him, 'Do you want us then to go and gather them up?' But he said, 'No, lest while you gather up the tares you also uproot the wheat with them. Let both grow together until the harvest, and at the time of harvest I will say to the reapers, "First gather together the tares and bind them in bundles to burn them, but gather the wheat into my barn"'" (vv. 27–30, NKJV).

A tare is a false grain. It looks like grain, but it actually has poisons in it and ruins the crop by choking out the good grain. In the Bible story the landowner says, "Hold on. First, gather the good stuff, then we will go back and get the bad crop and burn it." The same thing happens in the spirit. God says, "I am going to have to bring a separation. I am not doing it now because some of the crop is tangled up with the tares."

God wants us to be free from the things that so easily entangle us. Are you tangled up? I see a generation tangled up in the chains of this world. What seems like freedom now only leads to a life of pain. The prophet Jeremiah said it best: "We made our bed and now lie in it, all tangled up in the dirty sheets of dishonor. All because we sinned against our God, we and our fathers and mothers. From the time we took our first steps, said our first words, we've been rebels, disobeying the voice of our God" (Jer. 3:25, THE MESSAGE).

Mankind has been getting tangled in the wrong things since the Garden of Eden. Jesus came to bring a separation. He made a promise in Matthew 10:34: "Do not suppose that I have come to bring peace to the earth. I did not come to bring peace, but a sword." Jesus is saying that He is not only a God of peace and love but also a Savior who came to war on our behalf.

Here is a powerful wake-up call found in Revelation 3:1–3: "To the angel of the church in Sardis write…I know your deeds; you have a reputation of being alive, but you are dead. Wake up! Strengthen what remains and is about to die, for I have not found your deeds complete in the sight of my God. Remember, therefore, what you have received and heard; obey it, and repent. But if you do not wake up, I will come like a thief, and you will not know at what time I will come to you."

It is in darkness that we find ourselves in the most dangerous of circumstances. Most crimes do not happen in the day; they take place in the cover of night. It is in the light that things can no longer hide. We know that God is light and in Him there is no darkness (1 John 1:5), so why do we allow ourselves to live in dark places?

Believe it or not, God can see in our darkness. Proverbs 5:21–23 says, "Mark well that GOD doesn't miss a move you make; he's aware of every step you take. The shadow of your sin will overtake you; you'll find yourself stumbling all over yourself in the dark. Death is the reward of an undisciplined life; your foolish decisions trap you in a dead end" (THE MESSAGE).

The very first thing God did for creation was to create light! Genesis 1:3–4 says, "And God said, 'Let there be light,' and there was light. God saw that the light was good, and he separated the light from the darkness." God invaded the dark, but it is amazing how much darkness has invaded God's territory. Whether it is depression, fear, oppression, discouragement, or a lack of joy, freedom, or purpose, darkness seems to be around us on every side. In the next several pages I want to share what I like to call "light killers." These are the three things the devil sends to rob us of God's light.

LIGHT KILLER #1: DEPRESSION

Both physical and mental issues can lead to depression, but mostly it is caused by the weight and cares of life. Depression can roll in like a thick fog. Like a force from the pit of hell, it can take a person out of the game. Depression is a very real part of our culture. The National Institute of Mental Health reports that roughly 11 percent of adolescents have a depressive disorder by age eighteen.[1] And according to the Centers for Disease Control and Prevention, depression affects one in ten adults,[2] including about 6 million elderly people.[3]

I believe with all of my heart that God can deliver anyone walking through depression. After losing his family and his business, Job fell into a depression and wondered why he had ever been born. He told God, "I wish I had died before any eye saw me. If only I had never come into being, or had been carried straight from the womb to the grave! Are not my few days almost over? Turn away from me so I can have a moment's joy before I go to the place of no return, to the land of gloom and deep shadow, to the land of deepest night, of deep shadow and disorder, where even the light is like darkness" (Job 10:18–22).

Job was having a terrible time dealing with life. At the point of desperation Job was declaring, "Life is hard; life is consuming me! Why did I have to be born?" He was truly walking through a terrible place. He said, "Even light is like darkness."

Depression has a paralyzing effect. It can cause people to get stuck thinking things will never change. People are not called to walk through life in a cloud of depression. God is the God of joy and freedom. When depression hits, we must create atmospheres of freedom. Isaiah 60:1 tells us, "Arise [from the depression and prostration in which circumstances have kept you—rise to a new life]! Shine (be radiant with the glory of the Lord), for your light has come, and the glory of the Lord has risen upon you!" (AMP).

We must declare the goodness of God even when we don't feel good ourselves. We cannot be ruled by our emotions. We must continually thank God and praise Him for who He is, and that cloud of depression will have to move. Nehemiah said it best—"The joy of the LORD is your strength!" (Neh. 8:10).

Job walked through deep depression, but I don't believe he ever turned a deaf ear to God. He allowed God to teach him valuable lessons even in those dark times. The Bible says God "reveals the deep things of darkness and brings deep shadows into the light" (Job 12:22). Even in our darkest moments God will reveal Himself to us and show us His glory.

LIGHT KILLER #2: ANXIETY AND FEAR

The combination of anxiety and fear is the second light killer. When anxiety and fear take root in our lives, they have the power to stop our dreams and make us think there is no hope for our situation.

After the terrorist attacks on September 11, 2001, our nation seemed to be in a fog. On the Saturday after the attacks I was scheduled to fly to Memphis, Tennessee, to speak at a church. My flight was changed twice, and by the time I boarded the flight, it was very late. Everyone was on edge, and as I took my seat I noticed the flight attendant had been crying. As I looked at the other passengers, I could see the fear on their faces. People were wondering if they would make it to their destination or if there would be another attack.

I took a bold step and asked the flight attendant if I could pray over the plane. I explained that I was a Christian minister. What happened next was an absolute miracle. The flight attendant handed me the telephone and said, "Please pray over everyone." I took the phone and told everyone on the plane that I believed Christ could bring peace to all of us. Then I prayed and took my seat. A sense of calm came over the plane that was really unexplainable. It was late, and as I looked around the plane I saw people begin to fall asleep. When we landed in Memphis, it was very quiet. God had invaded the plane.

Isaiah 41 tells us, "Count on it: Everyone who had it in for you will end up out in the cold—real losers. Those who worked against you will end up empty-handed—nothing to show for their lives. When you go out looking for your old adversaries you won't find them—not a trace of your old enemies, not even a memory. That's right. Because I, your God, have a firm grip on you and I'm not letting go. I'm telling you, 'Don't panic. I'm right here to help you'" (vv. 11–13, THE MESSAGE).

When you are tempted to fear, you must remember that God is in control. He will never walk away from you, and He always has your back! He has a firm grip on you! Consider the following statistics about fear:

- Forty percent of what you worry about will never happen.

- Thirty percent of what you fear or worry about happened in the past and can't be changed.

- Ten percent of what we worry about is considered by most to be insignificant issues.

- Twelve percent of what we worry about is related to health problems that we will not encounter. This means that 92 percent of what we fear will never take place.

- Only 8 percent of what we worry about can be considered a legitimate concern.[4]

Our thoughts affect every aspect of our lives. Look what the apostle Paul said in Romans 8:6: "The mind of sinful man is death, but the mind controlled by the Spirit is life and peace." Paul went further when he told the Romans, "Do not conform any longer to the pattern of this world, but be transformed by the renewing of your mind. Then you will be able to test and approve what God's will is—his good, pleasing and perfect will" (Rom. 12:2).

It is God's will that we give Him not only our hearts and lives but also our minds. Fear and anxiety are abolished when you realize that God is in control. Let him change your mindset. You can walk in boldness to experience the life He has for you.

Light Killer #3: Hidden Sin

Ephesians 5:13–14 says, "But everything exposed by the light becomes visible, for it is light that makes everything visible. This is why it is said: 'Wake up, O sleeper, rise from the dead, and Christ will shine on you.'" It is natural to try to hide what is embarrassing to us. That is exactly what Adam and Eve did in the Garden of Eden when they disobeyed God. Our minds tell us that if we get real about what's going on in our lives, people will reject us. So we hide our issues, but sooner or later God loves us enough to bring hidden things to light.

God doesn't act like a child and run around telling on us to everyone. But by His very nature as the source of all truth, He must bring secret things into light. Psalms 18:28 says, "You, O LORD, keep my lamp burning; my God turns my darkness into light."

My greatest concern for my personal well-being is that I never get to a place where I no longer feel the sting of secret sin. When secret sin no longer affects our conscience, we have begun to enter into a slow and painful death. We all need a "gut check." This is when your spirit man says, "Stop what you are doing or it will destroy you!" It is a dangerous place to be when you no longer feel conviction for sin.

Anything done in secret always has a way of being exposed with a vengeance. The devil loves to convince people that everyone is doing it and God understands that we are all just human. The truth is that God will give us the strength to obey His rules. The devil loves to set people up for a fall. And the greater the person's influence, the more damage the sin will do to the body of Christ and the world watching us.

A dear mentor in my life named Jeanne Mayo always tells leaders, "Don't allow your gifts to take you where your character cannot keep you." That is good advice for all of us.

God sees everything. He doesn't use bifocals and separate people by status or prominence. Proverbs 15:11 says, "Even hell holds no secrets from God—do you think he can't read human hearts?" (THE MESSAGE). The Bible gives clear direction about what we must do when we sin—repent.

> This, in essence, is the message we heard from Christ and are passing on to you: God is light, pure light; there's not a trace of darkness in him. If we claim that we experience a shared life with him and continue to stumble around in the dark, we're obviously lying through our teeth—we're not living what we claim. But if we walk in the light, God himself being the light, we also experience a shared life with one another, as the sacrificed blood of Jesus, God's Son, purges all our sin. If we claim that we're free of sin, we're only fooling ourselves. A claim like that is errant nonsense. On the other hand, *if we admit our sins—make a clean breast of them—he won't let us down; he'll be true to himself. He'll forgive our sins and purge us of all wrongdoing.*
> —1 JOHN 1:5–9, THE MESSAGE, EMPHASIS ADDED

If we simply repent of our sins, God is faithful to forgive. We do not have to hide our sin in the dark. Stop hitting the snooze button! And don't let the time you spent in darkness go to waste—learn from it.

NO MORE HITTING THE SNOOZE BUTTON

In Isaiah 45:3 God says, "I will give you the treasures of darkness, riches stored in secret places, so that you may know that I am the LORD, the God of Israel, who summons you by name." God knows your name, and He wants to give you the treasures of darkness. All He wants is for you to wake yourself up.

Ephesians 4:22–24 says, "Since, then, we do not have the excuse of ignorance, everything—and I do mean everything—connected with that old way of life has to go. It's rotten through and through. Get rid of it! And then take on an entirely new way of life—a God-fashioned life, a life renewed from the inside and working itself into your conduct as God accurately reproduces his character in you" (THE MESSAGE). No more hitting the snooze button. Stop putting off what needs to be done today.

Psalm 36:9 says, "In your light we see light." It is time to separate the light from the darkness! Make right decisions about who God is in your life. Cry out to Him and ask Him to start a new work in you. I encourage you to take a moment now to get alone somewhere and ask God to change your life! We been given a great promise in Romans 10:9: "If you confess with your mouth, 'Jesus is Lord,' and believe in your heart that God raised him from the dead, you will be saved."

This is the moment for your freedom. All you have to do is pray the following prayer.

Dear Jesus, You know who I am. You have known me since my conception. You have a great plan for me. I am ready for a life of freedom in You. Today I invite You to be my Lord and Savior. I turn my back on my past and ask that You forgive me of all of my sin. I know You're not mad at me, and I know that You have a great plan for my life. Please help me to live according to Your Word. I know that You died for my sins, rose from the grave, and have a plan for me. So today I declare that Jesus Christ is Lord! Thank You for making me your child. In Jesus's name I pray, amen!

If you just prayed that prayer, you are a new creation in Christ—"the old has gone, the new has come!" (2 Cor. 5:17). Welcome to a new life of power, authority, and victory! That doesn't mean everything will magically become perfect, but you are promised you will never face anything alone. You are alive in Christ and now dead to the past! Welcome to the family!

Chapter 23

THIS IS NO EASY WALK

IT IS TIME for another great awakening in this nation! The cry for more of God is being heard around the land from bedrooms to churches to boardrooms. God's Spirit is sounding a clarion call to all who will listen. God is stirring people to get real for Him, and I am seeing people wake up. There are God movements taking place, and generations of people are running back to Christ! I have seen tens of thousands of people getting set free by the power of God. So many people are realizing it is OK to want more of God.

The fields are ripe for harvest! God is looking for workers. We must be the generation that takes back what the devil has stolen. We must declare His truth! It is the truth that sets people free (John 8:32). We have to realize there is something to sing about!

> At that same time, a fine vineyard will appear. There's something to sing about! I, God, tend it. I keep it well-watered. I keep careful watch over it so that no one can damage it. I'm not angry. I care. Even if it gives me thistles and thornbushes, I'll just pull them out and burn them up. Let that vine cling to me for safety, let it find a good and whole life with me, let it hold on for a good and whole life.
> —Isaiah 27:2–5, The Message

The scripture above is showing us the heart of God toward us. God is the master gardener, and He is at work tending His fields. God doesn't have time to be angry when His very nature is to nurture!

It is so easy to think God is mad at you when you spend your life looking in the mirror and never out the window. The truth is, in our Western culture life is pretty good. We go to bed each night to the sound of some pundit ranting on a twenty-four-hour news channel about the state of the union or some sports commentator bloviating about an overpaid athlete. In our culture God is often someone we mutter prayers to when we're taking a test in school, riding on a plane, or feeling guilty about watching something we knew wasn't good for us.

In chapter 1 I shared statistics on how Americans view God. Eighty-five percent of our nation sees God as authoritative, benevolent, critical, or distant. In other words, the very concept of God carries with it a stigma of control, aloofness, or plausible ineptness. Because of this view of God we find it easy to believe He might be mad at us. My goal in this chapter is to show you that Christianity is more than an opinion.

I am always amazed when I go overseas and see what God is doing in places with far fewer resources. In third world nations where life is so hard or it is illegal to be a Christian, the church is growing rapidly, and the believers are passionate. How can this be? Many would assume that people in countries rife with hardship, persecution, famine, and disease would think God is not good, but the opposite is often true.

There is a powerful ministry called Open Doors that has taken the gospel into some of the world's most hostile regions. On their website the group states that "over 100 million Christians worldwide suffer interrogation, arrest and even death for their faith, with millions more facing discrimination and alienation."[1] In many Muslim countries just being caught with a Bible could mean losing your head. In December 2011 forty-two Ethiopian Christians were arrested in Saudi Arabia simply for being followers of Christ.[2] And during Egypt's Arab Spring (and Israel's winter), churches in Cairo were burned, vandalized, and violated. In a commentary posted by *The Australian*, author Micah Halpern wrote at the time that the world was relatively silent "as Egypt's Muslims systematically...set about massacring Egypt's Christians."[3]

Communist China is one of the most closed countries to Christianity, yet the church there is exploding. *The Economist* reported in 2008 that the number of Christians in China could be anywhere from 21 million (the Chinese government's estimate) to 70 million according to the Centre for the Study of Global Christianity in Massachusetts to 130 million according to Chinese church leaders. Since the statistics were reported, the numbers have only continued to increase.[4]

Churches in China are growing despite the threat of intimidation, arrest, and persecution. *It simply doesn't make sense.* Why would they take risks to worship a God who would allow them to be martyred, imprisoned, or tortured? Maybe they know something we don't know. Could it be that God is more than just a Santa Claus–type figure, more than a two-hour weekend commitment, more than the mascot for a voting block? One pastor from Shanghai who lives his life on the edge for Jesus said if the head of one house church was arrested, "the congregation would just split up and might break into five, six or even ten new house churches."[5] The millions who serve God in nations where it is dangerous to be a Christian must realize something about God's character we need to know.

GOD WANTS ALL OF YOU

In October 2011 I was in Singapore speaking to a group of students and leaders. The room was packed mostly with Asian believers. In the midst of my lesson I asked, "How many of you are first-generation Christians in your home?" I was amazed as nearly 90 percent of the hands went up. I stood silently as tears filled my eyes at the sight of these beautiful young saints.

I knew what this meant. It meant that each evening they returned to their homes and apartments having to face older family members who had no idea about the God these warriors served. It meant walking past statues of Buddha or Hindu gods as they settled in for the evening. Yet for these young believers this was just a normal part of life. They believe God is worth everything they have to give up or endure in order to have a relationship with Him.

I love what the great missionary Jim Elliot, who was martyred for his faith, said, "He is no fool who gives up what he cannot keep to gain that which he cannot lose."[6] You see, I have learned that if a person thinks the cost is too great, then God's calling is not enough to sustain him! God desires and expects to have every part of our beings! He wants us to be enraptured in Him!

What would cause people to sacrifice everything for God? What would cause missionaries to leave the comfort of their homes, sell everything, and head to the dark regions of the world? Maybe they take Jesus's words in Matthew 28:19–20 seriously: "Therefore go and make disciples of all nations, baptizing them in the name of the Father and of the Son and of the Holy Spirit, and teaching them to obey everything I have commanded you."

That is the mandate of the called! John Keith Falconer made a powerful statement when he said, "I have but one candle of life to burn, and I would rather burn it out in a land filled with darkness than in a land flooded with light."[7] Could it be that God is so much more than we can imagine, that His love and power exceed our imagination? Could it be that God has lands and territories for you to invade? The Bible declares in Acts 17:26 that from one man He made all the nations, that they should inhabit the whole earth, and He marked out their appointed times in history and the boundaries of their lands.

God has already determined where you will walk and live. You are called to occupy territory! There may be tough roads ahead of you, but God is with you. Recently, I heard Prophet Cindy Jacobs make this statement: "If you are going into your promised land and not facing giants, then you're just a tourist!"[8]

God is calling us to be His hands extended. We are called to change things. One of the greatest quotes I have ever read is by St. Augustine: "Hope has two beautiful daughters; their names are anger and courage; anger at the way things are, and courage to see that they do not remain the way they are."[9] We must allow anger and courage to push us out of our comfort zone. Why live in a box instead of the land you've been called to possess?

I shared all of this to stir your heart and spirit. I want you to understand that Christianity is more than a church service, a gathering of Sunday morning saints, or a social club of the redeemed. It is so much more than we can imagine. Christianity is about understanding that a loving God—who likes you, dreams with you, and sent His Son to die on a cross for you—has a plan for your life.

If God were mad at us, would all of the persecution in the world be worth enduring? Absolutely not! In all other religions of the world mankind added his opinions and preferences to craft the kind of deity he wanted. Man made the rules and was able to fulfill his own fantasies, determine what must be sacrificed, and determine who could be involved in the religion. But man cannot save himself. He can never give himself peace, joy, or security; he cannot redeem himself from the penalty of sin.

In Christianity God sent His Son to take care of everything man could never accomplish. I have a quote on the wall of my study that reminds me that I must go after the lost. I pray it will stir your heart.

> "Not *called*," did you say? Not *heard* the call, I think you should say. He has been calling loudly ever since He spoke your sins forgiven—if you are forgiven at all—entreating and beseeching you to be His ambassador. Put your ear down to the Bible, and hear Him bid you go and pull sinners out of the fire of sin. Put your ear down to the burdened, agonized heart of humanity, and listen to its pitying wail for help. Go and stand by the gates of Hell, and hear the damned entreat you to go to their father's house, and bid their brothers, and sisters, and servants, and masters not to come there. And then look the Christ in the face, whose mercy you professed to have got, and tell Him whether you will join us heart and soul and body and circumstances in the march to publish His mercy to all the world.[10]
> —GENERAL WILLIAM BOOTH, FOUNDER OF THE
> SALVATION ARMY

I often share a passage from Hebrews 10 when speaking to young ministry students. In fact, Hebrews 10, 11, and 12 all remind us of our responsibility and purpose in Christ. I wanted to share the passage of Scripture below because it declares who and what we are called to be.

> Remember those earlier days after you had received the light, when you stood your ground in a great contest in the face of suffering. Sometimes you were publicly exposed to insult and persecution; at other times you stood side by side with those who were so treated. You sympathized with those in prison and joyfully accepted the confiscation of your property, because you knew that you yourselves had better and lasting possessions. So do not throw away your confidence; it

will be richly rewarded. You need to persevere so that when you have done the will of God, you will receive what he has promised. For in just a very little while, "He who is coming will come and will not delay. But my righteous one will live by faith. And if he shrinks back, I will not be pleased with him." But we are not of those who shrink back and are destroyed, but of those who believe and are saved.

—HEBREWS 10:32–39

Whatever you do, don't throw away your confidence! Hang in there. God isn't mad at you—no, He is mad about you! He is simply asking you to take a step and do what He asks. Luke 9:23 says, "Then he said to them all: 'If anyone would come after me, he must deny himself and take up his cross daily and follow me.'" We are not promised that this walk will be easy, but we are called to let the light of God's glory shine through us, so others can see what God has called them to be in Him!

This is not the end but really your beginning!

NOTES

INTRODUCTION

1. "Cutting Statistics and Self-Injury Treatment," TeenHelp .com, http://www.teenhelp.com/teen-health/cutting-stats-treat ment.html (accessed August 27, 2012).

CHAPTER 1
A CULTURE FULL OF NOISE

1. Friedrich Nietzsche, *The Gay Science*, trans. Walter Kaufmann (New York: Vintage Books/Random House, 1974).

2. Walter Kaufmann, *Nietzsche: Philosopher, Psychologist, Antichrist* (Princeton, NJ: Princeton University Press, 1974).

3. Robert Wicks, "Friedrich Nietzsche," *The Stanford Encyclopedia of Philosophy* http://plato.stanford.edu/entries/ nietzsche/#Lif184190 (accessed August 28, 2012).

4. Josh McDowell, Twitter.com, December 9, 2011.

5. Times Staff. "The 25 Most Influential Evangelicals in America," *Time* magazine, February 7, 2005, http://www.time .com/time/specials/packages/article/0,28804,1993235 _1993243_1993267,00.html (accessed August 28, 2012).

6. Tony Zuniga as quoted by Lisa Weidknecht in "Top Five Influences in a Child's Life," *Planet Weidknecht* blog, July 8, 2011, http://www.weidknecht.com/2011/07/top-five-influences-in -childs-life.html (accessed August 28, 2012).

7. Manali Oak, "Negative and Positive Effects of Peer Pressure," Buzzle.com, March 6, 2012, http://www.buzzle.com/ articles/negative-and-positive-effects-of-peer-pressure.html (accessed August 31, 2012).

8. Laurie Goodstein, "More Atheists Shout It From the Rooftops," *The New York Times*, April 26, 2009, http://www.nytimes.com/2009/04/27/us/27atheist.html (accessed August 28, 2012).

9. Ibid.

10. C. S. Lewis, *The Problem of Pain* (New York, NY: Harper Collins Publishers, 2001), 46. Viewed at Google Books.

11. Coexistbumpersticker.org, "Coexist Bumper Sticker Meaning" (accessed September 6, 2012).

12. Paul Froese and Christopher Bader, *America's Four Gods* (New York: Oxford University Press, Inc., 2010), 24–26. Viewed at Google Books.

CHAPTER 2
THE TRUTH ABOUT NATURAL DISASTERS

1. US Department of Commerce, *Service Assessment: The Historic Tornadoes of April 2011*, National Weather Service, December 2011, http://www.nws.noaa.gov/os/assessments/pdfs/historic_tornadoes.pdf (accessed August 28, 2012).

2. Adam Hamilton, "Japan's Earthquake and the Will of God," *Huffington Post*, March 21, 2011, http://www.huffingtonpost.com/adam-hamilton/was-japans-earthquake-the_b_837324.html (accessed August 28, 2012).

3. Ibid.

4. Sheila Marikar, "Glenn Beck Calls Japan Earthquake Work of God; Gilbert Gottfried Apologizes," ABC News, http://abcnews.go.com/Entertainment/glenn-beck-calls-japan-quake-message-god-gilbert/story?id=13139648#.UB_A1PZlT6k (accessed August 28, 2012).

CHAPTER 3
GOD IS A GOOD FATHER

1. David Rennie, "How's Your 'Progenitor A'?", *The Telegraph*, March 7, 2006, http://www.telegraph.co.uk/news/worldnews/europe/spain/1512344/Hows-your-Progenitor-A.html (accessed August 29, 2012).

2. US Census Bureau, "Custodial Mothers and Fathers and Their Child Support: 2009," Issued December 2011, http://www.census.gov/prod/2011pubs/p60-240.pdf, accessed June 28, 2012.

3. National Fatherhood Initiative, *Father Facts*, 5th edition, 2007, viewed at http://www.familyfoundationfund.org/ thefactsofthefatherless (accessed August 29, 2012).

4. National Center for Fathering, "The Consequences of Fatherlessness," http://www.fathers.com/content/index .php?option=com_content&task=view&id=391 (accessed August 29, 2012).

5. US Department of Justice, *What Can the Government Do to Decrease Crime and Revitalize Communities?*, https://www.ncjrs .gov/txtfiles/172210.txt (accessed August 29, 2012).

6. Ibid.

Chapter 5
God Is Not an Absentee Father

1. Denise Frangipane, *Overcoming Fear* (Cedar Rapids, IA: Arrow Publications, 1996), 11, as quoted in "My Journey," Ministries of Francis Frangipane, http://tinyurl.com/8gqf6sm (accessed August 29, 2012).

2. Glen Berteau, in communication with the author, October 1998.

Chapter 7
God Allows Us to Choose

1. John Calvin, *Institutes on the Christian Religion*, trans. Henry Beveridge (Peabody, MA: Hendrickson Publishers Inc., 2008), 475. Viewed at Google Books.

Chapter 8
God Doesn't Think the Way We Do

1. ThinkExist.com, St. Augustine Quotes, http://thinkexist .com/quotation/god-is-not-what-you-imagine-or-what-you-think -you/697103.html (accessed August 30, 2012).

2. Sculley Bradley, Harold W. Blodgett, Arthur Golden, et al., eds. *Leaves of Grass: A Textual Variorum of Poems* (New York: New York University Press, 1980).

CHAPTER 11
GOD DISCIPLINES THOSE HE LOVES

1. John Cloud and Henry Townsend, *Boundaries* (Grand Rapids, MI: Zondervan, 1992).

CHAPTER 12
GOD WANTS US TO BE BLESSED

1. "Unemployment Rate on the Rise in Half of U.S. Cities," *Huffington Post*, August 29, 2012, http://www.huffingtonpost.com/2012/08/30/unemployment-rate-on-the-rise-half-of-us-cities_n_1842555.html (accessed August 30, 2012).

2. "Number of Americans on Food Stamps Hits Another High Years After Recession's End," *Huffington Post*, November 3, 2011, http://www.huffingtonpost.com/2011/11/03/number-of-americans-on-snap_n_1074344.html (accessed August 30, 2012).

3. Pat Schatzline, "Is Jesus America's Mascot?", (blog), Mercy Seat Ministries, August 3, 2011, http://patschatzline.blogspot.com/2011/08/3m-9-is-jesus-americas-mascot.html (accessed August 30, 2012).

4. Andrew Taylor, "In God We Trust: Why Congress Reaffirmed the US Motto," Associated Press, November 3, 2011, http://www.csmonitor.com/USA/Latest-News-Wires/2011/1103/In-God-We-Trust-Why-Congress-reaffirmed-the-US-motto (accessed August 30, 2012).

5. Schatzline, "Is Jesus America's Mascot?"

6. Pastor George Sawyer in a sermon at Calvary Assembly of God, Decatur, Alabama, July 24, 2012.

7. TanBible.com, "Giving: Story of a Dollar," http://www.tanbible.com/tol_ill/giving.htm (accessed September 4, 2012).

8. "Winston Churchill quotes," ThinkExist.com, http://thinkexist.com/quotation/we_make_a_living_by_what_we_get-but_we_make_a/14355.html (accessed August 30, 2012).

CHAPTER 13
GOD IS CHEERING FOR US

1. Father Ron Shirley, "God the Cheerleader," (blog), FatherRon.com, May 29, 2011.

CHAPTER 14
TERRIBLE THINGS HAVE HAPPENED TO ME

1. C. S. Lewis, *The Problem of Pain* (New York: Harper One, 2001).

2. ChristiaNet.com, "Could God Be Mad at Me?", June 19, 2005, http://christianblogs.christianet.com/1119228308.htm (accessed September 4, 2012).

3. GodVine.com, "Clarke's Commentary on Romans 8:28," http://www.godvine.com/bible/Romans/8-28 (accessed September 4, 2012).

4. Ibid.

CHAPTER 15
GOD MADE A MISTAKE WHEN HE CREATED ME

1. Kendra Cherry, "What Is Cognitive Dissonance," About .com, http://psychology.about.com/od/cognitivepsychology/f/dissonance.htm (accessed September 4, 2012); Leon Festinger, *A Theory of Cognitive Dissonance* (Stanford, CA: Stanford University Press, 1957).

2. Michael Luo and Christina Capecchi, "Lutheran Group Eases Limits on Gay Clergy, *New York Times*, August 21, 2009, http://www.nytimes.com/2009/08/22/us/22lutherans.html (accessed September 4, 2012).

3. Matthew Moore, "Ben and Jerry's Renames Ice Cream Hubby Hubby in Celebration of Gay Marriage," *The Telegraph*, September 2, 2009, http://www.telegraph.co.uk/news/newstopics/howaboutthat/6125277/Ben-and-Jerrys-renames-ice-cream-Hubby-Hubby-in-celebration-of-gay-marriage.html (accessed September 4, 2012).

4. "President Obama Names Medal of Freedom Recipients," White House Press Office, July 30, 2009, http://www.whitehouse.gov/the_press_office/President-Obama-Names-Medal-of-Freedom-Recipients (accessed August 6, 2012).

5. Ibid.

6. Press Conference by the President, White House Press Office, June 29, 2011, http://www.whitehouse.gov/the-press

-office/2011/06/29/press-conference-president (accessed August 6, 2012).

7. ABC News, "President Obama Affirms His Support for Same Sex Marriage" http://abcnews.go.com/WNT/video/president-obama-affirms-support-gay-marriage-abc-news-16313266 (accessed October 4, 2012).

8. Sy Rogers, speaking at Jeanne Mayo's National Youth Leaders' Conference, March 13-14, 2012, Atlanta, Georgia.

9. Ibid.

10. Box Office Mojo, *The Hunger Games*, http://boxofficemojo.com/movies/?page=weekend&id=hungergames.htm (accessed September 4, 2012).

11. Rogers, speaking at Jeanne Mayo's National Youth Leaders' Conference.

12. Ibid.

13. As quoted in "Born or Bred: Science Does Not Support the Claim That Homosexuality Is Genetic" by Robert Knight, Concerned Women for America, http://www.cwfa.org/images/content/bornorbred.pdf (accessed September 4, 2012).

14. Samuele Bacchiocchi, *The Marriage Covenant: A Biblical Study on Marriage, Divorce, and Remarriage*, (n.p.: Biblical Perspectives, 2006).

15. David W. Purcell, Jocelyn D. Patterson, and Pilgrim S. Spikes Jr., "Childhood Sexual Abuse Experienced by Gay and Bisexual Men: Understanding the Disparities and Interventions to Help Eliminate Them," in Richard J. Wolitski, Ron Stall, and Ronald O Valdiserri, eds. *Unequal Opportunity* (Oxford: Oxford University Press, 2008), 72-96, as quoted by Jeff Johnson in "Childhood Sexual Abuse and Homosexuality," CitizenLink.com, June 17, 2010, http://www.citizenlink.com/2010/06/17/childhood-sexual-abuse-and-male-homosexuality/ (accessed September 4, 2012).

16. Centers for Disease Control and Prevention, "HIV among Gay and Bisexual Men," http://www.cdc.gov/hiv/topics/msm/index.htm (accessed September 4, 2012).

17. Centers for Disease Control and Prevention, "Gay and Bisexual Men's Health: Sexually Transmitted Diseases," http://www.cdc.gov/msmhealth/STD.htm (accessed September 4, 2012).

18. Covenant Baptist Dayton, "The Summation of All Things in Christ," http://www.covenantbaptistdayton.org/studies/Meadows/Ephesians/Eph11_ch2_vs4-10.pdf (accessed September 4, 2012).

19. Rogers, speaking at Jeanne Mayo's National Youth Leaders' Conference.

Chapter 16
My Church Teaches That God Is Angry

1. Joel Osteen, *Your Best Life Now* (New York: Warner Faith Books, 2004).

Chapter 17
I've Made Too Many Mistakes

1. Charles Spurgeon, "All of Grace," Sermon No. 3479, published October 7, 1915, http://www.spurgeon.org/sermons/3479.htm (accessed September 5, 2012).

2. Concordances.org, Strong's Concordance and HELPS Word-studies, http://concordances.org/greek/5485.htm (accessed September 5, 2012).

Chapter 18
God Allowed Me to Get Sick

1. Reinhard Bonnke in communication with the author, January 2012.

2. Ibid.

3. Blue Letter Bible. "Dictionary and Word Search for *sōtēria* (Strong's 4991)," http://www.blueletterbible.org/LANG/LEXICON/lexicon.cfm?Strongs=G4991&cscs=Jhn (accessed September 5, 2012).

Chapter 19
The Devil Is a Liar!

1. Thayer's Greek Lexicon, Electronic Database. Copyright © 2002, 2003, 2006, 2011 by Biblesoft, Inc. All rights reserved. Used by permission. http://concordances.org/greek/2725.htm(accessed October 4, 2012).

2. Blue Letter Bible. "Dictionary and Word Search for *diablos* (Strong's 1228)," http://www.blueletterbible.org/lang/lexicon/ lexicon.cfm?strongs=G1228 (accessed September 5, 2012).

3. Glyn Barrett, *If I Was the Devil* (Kent, England: Sovereign World Ltd, 2004).

CHAPTER 22
IT'S TIME TO WAKE UP!

1. National Institute of Mental Health, "Major Depressive Disorder in Children," http://www.nimh.nih.gov/ statistics/1MDD_CHILD.shtml (accessed September 6, 2012); National Institute of Mental Health, "Depression in Children and Adolescents (Fact Sheet)," http://www.nimh.nih.gov/health/ publications/depression-in-children-and-adolescents/index.shtml (accessed September 6, 2012).

2. Centers for Disease Control and Prevention, "An Estimated 1 in 10 U.S. Adults Report Depression," http://www.cdc.gov/ features/dsdepression/index.html (accessed September 6, 2012).

3. WebMD.com, "Depression in the Elderly," http://www .webmd.com/depression/guide/depression-elderly (accessed September 6, 2012).

4. FearofStuff.com, "Fear's Amazing Statistics," http://www .fearofstuff.com/featured/fears-amazing-statistics/ (accessed September 6, 2012).

CHAPTER 23
THIS IS NO EASY WALK

1. Open Doors, "FAQ About Open Doors USA," http://www .opendoorsusa.org/about-us/faq (accessed September 6, 2012).

2. International Christian Concern, "42 Ethiopian Christians Arrested in Saudi Arabia," December 17 2011, http://www .persecution.org/2011/12/17/42-ethiopian-christians-arrested-in -saudi-arabia/ (accessed September 6, 2012).

3. Micah Halpern, "Coptic Christians Slaughtered in Egypt as the World Looks Away," *The Australian*, May 16, 2011, http:// www.theaustralian.com.au/news/opinion/coptic -christians-slaughtered-in-egypt-as-the-world-looks-away/story -e6frg6zo-1226056354274 (accessed September 6, 2012).

4. "Inside China's Fastest-Growing Non-Governmental Organisation, *The Economist*, October 2, 2008, http://www.economist.com/node/12342509 (accessed September 6, 2012).

5. Ibid.

6. Elisabeth Elliot, *In The Shadow of the Almighty* (New York: HarperCollins Publisher, 1958), 108.

7. Southern Nazarene University, "Missions Slogans and Notables Quotes From Missionaries," http://home.snu.edu/~hculbert/slogans.htm (accessed September 6, 2012).

8. Love Your City Conference, Trinity Church, Cedar Hill, Texas, September 11, 2012.

9. Beliefnet.com, Inspirational Quotes, http://www.beliefnet.com/Quotes/Christian/S/St-Augustine/Hope-Has-Two-Beautiful-Daughters-Their-Names-Are.aspx (accessed September 6, 2012).

10. William Booth, *The General's Letters, 1885* (London: The Salvation Army, 1890), 4–5. Viewed at Google Books.

ABOUT THE AUTHOR

PAT SCHATZLINE IS one of America's leading communicators and evangelists to students and adults. Pat and his wife, Karen, cofounded Mercy Seat Ministries in 1997. Since then Pat and Karen have ministered to more than two million people as they have traveled the globe ministering God's love and power at churches, conferences, camps, retreats, and universities.

Pat has been the keynote speaker at some of the largest youth church conferences in the world. He is known for his crazy humor, his unique ability to communicate God's Word with passion, and his deep desire to see a generation of youth and adults experience the amazing love and power of God. Through the demonstration of God's power during altar calls, tens of thousands of lives have been transformed during Pat's meetings.

In 2012 Pat and Karen founded the Legacy Conferences, through which they mentor leaders across the nation. They also are the founders of the Forerunner School of Ministry, which has launched hundreds into full-time ministry since it began in 2001. Hundreds listen to Pat's weekly podcast, and he has been featured on Christian television programs such as JCTV and TBN's *Praise the Lord*, as well as in magazines and newspapers.

Married for twenty-two years, Pat and Karen have two children, Nate and Abby, and one daughter-in-law, Adrienne. They live in Birmingham, Alabama.

EMPOWERED
TO RADICALLY CHANGE
YOUR WORLD

Charisma House brings you books, e-books, and other media from dynamic Spirit-filled Christians who are passionate about God.

Check out all of our releases from best-selling authors like **Jentezen Franklin**, **Perry Stone**, and **Joseph Prince** and experience God's supernatural power at work.

CHARISMA
HOUSE

www.charismahouse.com
twitter.com/charismahouse • facebook.com/charismahouse